PRAISE FOR *HUMAN CENTERED MARKETING*

"All effective marketing is human-centered. While we're busy being distracted with shortcuts, Faus helps us refocus on what matters."
Seth Godin, author of *This is Marketing*

"Trust is under siege from nearly every angle, yet marketers like you and me want (need!) to build trust with our audiences. The question is, how? Ashley Faus draws you a map."
Ann Handley, best-selling author and Chief Content Officer, MarketingProfs

"Most of the go-to playbooks are outdated, but it's hard to find a replacement for stale marketing practices. Ashley Faus constructed a powerful new set of frameworks, along with practical advice and real-world examples. *Human-Centered Marketing* brings us back to what actually matters: The people behind the screen."
Nancy Duarte, best-selling author and CEO of Duarte, Inc.

"Enterprises love the idea of transformation, but do they have the execution chops? Often, the answer is no. Ashley Faus's proven mix of actionable marketing frameworks plus slide-ready metrics are spot-on for today's big, complex organizations."
Heike Young, Head of Content & Integrated Marketing, Microsoft

"Business transformation doesn't happen through finger-pointing, it happens in teams, with the right frameworks. In this book, Ashley Faus shares powerful, practical frameworks to drive clarity, alignment, and trust—turning your team into a high-performing go-to-market powerhouse."
Sangram Vajre, Terminus and former CMO of Pardot, and *Wall Street Journal* best-selling author

"As a CMO operating in an era of declining trust, very few marketing books offer practical insights into how company brands can build trust by tapping into the human element and the person-to-person connection. Ashley Faus's book provides a unique collection of rich frameworks and real-world case studies that show brands how to keep humans at the center of their marketing."
Kerry-Ann Betton Stimpson, CMO and *Forbes* Communications Council Member

"The frameworks Ashley Faus shares are a game-changer for PMMs, especially those working at the enterprise level. Her playground mindset challenges outdated funnel thinking, encouraging PMMs to embrace a more holistic approach to channels and thought leadership. These insights are not just innovative but essential for anyone looking to elevate their impact in Product Marketing."
Mary Sheehan, author of *The Pocket Guide to Product Launches*

"When I need marketing advice, Ashley Faus is one of my top people to go to. In *Human-Centered Marketing*, Faus has masterfully captured the evolution of modern marketing. Her insights challenge outdated funnel-driven approaches, replacing them with trust-based, audience-first frameworks that align with how people actually engage today. This book is a must-read for any marketer looking to build long-term relationships and brand credibility in the AI era."
Morgan J. Ingram, Founder and CEO, AMP Creative

"This isn't just another marketing book—it's a much-needed wake-up call. Ashley Faus challenges outdated norms and introduces frameworks that make human connection the cornerstone of marketing. *Human-Centered Marketing* is THE blueprint to meaningful engagement and measurable results. In a world of AI, may we all be more human-centered!"
Hattie the PMM, Founder, productmarketers.com

Human-Centered Marketing

How to Connect with Audiences in the Age of AI

Ashley Faus

First published in Great Britain and the United States in 2025 by Kogan Page Limited

Kogan Page

Kogan Page Ltd, 2nd Floor, 45 Gee Street, London EC1V 3RS, United Kingdom
Kogan Page Inc, 8 W 38th Street, Suite 90, New York, NY 10018, USA
www.koganpage.com

EU Representative (GPSR)

Authorised Rep Compliance Ltd, Ground Floor, 71 Baggot Street Lower, Dublin D02 P593, Ireland
www.arccompliance.com

Kogan Page books are printed on paper from sustainable forests.

ISBNs

Hardback	978 1 3986 1940 1
Paperback	978 1 3986 1938 8
Ebook	978 1 3986 1939 5

British Library Cataloguing-in-Publication Data

A CIP record for this book is available from the British Library.

Library of Congress Control Number

2025932692

Typeset by Integra Software Services, Pondicherry
Print production managed by Jellyfish
Printed and bound by CPI Group (UK) Ltd, Croydon CR0 4YY

CONTENTS

LIST OF FIGURES
AND TABLE

Figures

Table

FOREWORD

Marketing today feels like being trapped in a constant loop of chasing metrics, optimizing for algorithms, and checking off content-sharing boxes. We've all seen it: the race to automate everything, pump out more content, and measure every single touchpoint to drive one thing—revenue. But, somewhere in all this, we've lost sight of the very thing marketing is supposed to be about: people. That's where Ashley Faus comes in, reminding us of one fundamental truth—people trust people, not AI bots, and certainly not meaningless vanity metrics.

But how do we put people, or, more importantly, humanity, into our marketing and sales process, and is this something that we can even measure?

The traditional marketing funnel is dead. Social media can't just be another place to dump links, and "thought leadership" often feels like corporate buzzword garbage. But, even knowing that, we still cling to those old models because they're safe and familiar, and, let's face it, change is hard. What Ashley offers in this book is not just a critique of the old way of doing things; she's codified a new approach. She's proven it works and is willing to help others find their way off the hamster wheel of automated nonsense and onto a more human-centered approach.

This book isn't just another "let's disrupt marketing" manifesto—it's a playbook filled with practical frameworks, real-world examples, and a deep understanding of what it means to truly connect with an audience. Ashley's willingness to say what needs to be said based on real experience from an incredible career journey, combined with her ability to back it up with results, makes her the exact person you want guiding you through this shift.

Ashley didn't write this book just because it's trendy to talk about "putting humans back in marketing." She wrote it because she believes in it down to her core. When she talks about focusing on the humans behind the screen, it's not just lip service. She lives this stuff.

She's spent years testing her frameworks with the biggest brands on the planet, debating them on stages at the biggest events in the industry, and working across every sector and company size. From start-ups to global enterprises, she's been in the trenches and has helped teams navigate the complexities of modern marketing with a focus on real human connection.

So, what's this book all about? It's about trust. It's about connection. It's about finding a way to cut through the noise of automation, AI, and endless tracking to actually reach people where they are—with content that speaks to their needs, not just their wallets. And Ashley doesn't stop at theory. She gives you the tools to make it happen, with frameworks like the Playground Model for mapping audience journeys, the Social Media Spectrum for engaging authentically, and the Four Pillars of Thought Leadership for building trust over time.

Marketing doesn't have to be a game of throwing more tech at the problem or chasing the next shiny trend. It can be about people, relationships, and trust. Humanity in the marketing and sales process will not come from tweaking your automation streams or a slick new piece of content... It is a change in mindset. The frameworks here aren't just ideas—they're battle-tested strategies that can help you build long-term growth by focusing on what really matters: the humans behind the screen.

If you're tired of feeling like a cog in the machine, and you're ready to ditch the linear funnel and embrace a more fluid, human-centered approach, then you're in the right place. Ashley's not only the right person to take you on this journey—she's been where you are, and she knows exactly how to help you succeed.

Jay Schwedelson, Founder and CEO, GURU Media Hub

ACKNOWLEDGMENTS

Writing a book often feels like a solo journey, but there are many companions and fellow travelers along the way. I'm grateful for all the support, commiseration, and cheering as I charged up this hill.

First, I want to thank my husband for his enthusiastic support of this pursuit. He was excited when I signed the contract, frustrated on my behalf when I had a touch of writer's block, and proud when I turned in the final manuscript. He's been excited to tell friends, family, and colleagues about the book, and I know he'll be the first person to show up at the launch party (and let's be honest... he'll be there to help set up a table full of signed books, snagging his own copy for reference). It's truly something special to share this milestone with him.

Second, I want to thank the team at Kogan Page. From helping me hone the proposal, to editing and fact-checking, to design and layout, the team has been so helpful. By the time the book release happens, we'll have been traveling together for over a year, and it's been wonderful to have the team on this journey. I'm excited to keep working together to promote the book and enjoy the success!

Third, I want to thank all the smart people featured in the book. You did the hard work of researching, thinking, implementing, and measuring all your programs and solutions, and you shared that work with the world in a meaningful way. Thank you for the conversations, the reports, the videos, and the sparring throughout this process. I'm honored to amplify your work throughout the book.

Finally, I want to thank the early readers and supporters who provided endorsements and offered to support the launch of the book. From helping me think through the outline, to consulting on the contract, to offering quotes about the impact of the book, I'm fortunate to have a strong network of friends—not just colleagues or professional contacts, but true friends who were excited to join me on this journey. I feel supported and celebrated by the people who were willing to read early drafts, give their stamp of approval by providing a name and quote, and volunteering to spread the word about my frameworks and, ultimately, the book.

Though the writing is a solo endeavor, it turns out that the journey is not lonely at all. I'm honored to have such traveling companions, and I hope to return the favor as you all chase your goals!

Trust: The Foundation That Fuels Business Outcomes

Who Do You Trust?

Business is built on trust, and people trust people like themselves. As marketers, we need to understand the foundations of trust in order to win the hearts, minds, and wallets of our audience. We must speak the language of the audience, deeply understand their needs, and, ultimately, show, not tell, people how we can solve their challenges.

My husband and I decided to celebrate our 15th wedding anniversary in Palm Springs, California. I was so excited to plan our trip, complete with fancy dinners, dressy outfits, and craft cocktails.

First, I decided to use Google to plan the trip, searching "best restaurants in Palm Springs" and "couples vacation in Palm Springs."

The results were overwhelming.

- Which restaurant is the best?
- Which hike is the best?
- Which spa is the best?

So, I decided to ask ChatGPT to help me figure out the best itinerary for a long weekend. I typed in the prompts, "Recommend restaurants in Palm Springs for an anniversary dinner" and "Create a 3-day itinerary for an active couple celebrating a wedding anniversary." The results were bland and included many of the same standard suggestions shown in the Google search.

Then, I remembered that my co-worker had recently married in Palm Springs. I asked her for recommendations, and she sent me a carefully curated list with her insider comments about where to stay, where to eat, and what to do.

It was perfect, and we ended up having a lovely weekend, enjoying many of the spots she had recommended.

Why were her individual suggestions so much better than Google or ChatGPT? Why did I trust her more than hundreds of random strangers on the internet, or a mysterious algorithm powering an answer from a large language model?

Because she's like me.

She's in a dual income, no kids (DINK) household, celebrating love and lifelong commitment, with lifestyle activities and food preferences that are similar to my own. Armed with nothing but her own personal experience, her list cut through the noise and decision-making. Her language to describe each location, activity, and restaurant was specific and useful to me, personally.

While the internet is great at gathering information, it's not great at knowing individuals. It doesn't understand our moment-by-moment quirks, whims, and contradictory desires.

We can automate, outsource, and hack a lot of things. But human connection? That's still real.

Trust Trends

I'm not alone in feeling overwhelmed, skeptical, and slightly distrust-ful of information on the internet. In fact, in 2018, the Edelman Trust Barometer noted that nearly 7 out of 10 survey respondents worried about false information or fake news being used as a weapon, and that "media" was the least-trusted institution.[1]

The report included a follow-up question about the definition of "media", and found that it included social media platforms, news applications, search platforms, and content publishers including brands, influencers, and journalists.

This trend continued in the 2019 report, with trust as low as 34 per cent among respondents when asked how much they trust search engines, traditional media, and social media as a source of news.[2] Reports from 2020 and subsequent years continue to show declining trust in traditional publishing outlets and markers of authority, such as a leadership role in a business or government position.[3]

Despite the overall decline in trust, some groups remained steady or made gains over the years. In 2023, the report found that businesses are more trusted (62 per cent) than non-government organizations (NGOs) (59 per cent), government (50 per cent), and the media (50 per cent). It also found that "my neighbors", "my CEO", and "my co-workers" are more trusted than generic CEOs, journalists, or government officials.[4] In 2024, 74 per cent of respondents said they trust "someone like me", and 66 per cent said they trust a "company technical expert."[5]

Trust is not a fluffy or ethereal feeling; it has real economic impact. The 2022 Edelman Trust report found that:

- 58 per cent of respondents bought from or advocated for brands based on their beliefs and values
- 60 per cent chose a place of work based on their beliefs and values
- 64 per cent invested based on their beliefs and values.[6]

Building trust and rapport through shared identity, values, and beliefs results in increased economic outcomes, from short-term sales, to attracting qualified workers, to shareholder investment.

Changes Impacting Trust

We've seen the trends in trust, but what is behind the overall decline, and the few pockets of continued or increased trust?

While artificial intelligence (AI) and automation capabilities are climbing the hype curve, this shift started decades ago. In fact, Edelman summarized its 2005 Trust Barometer with this headline: "Trust shifts from 'authorities' to peers."[7]

With the rise of the internet, audiences moved away from local sources of information, and began consuming more from online sources. If audiences move online, we know marketers are sure to follow, intent on finding ways to reach potential buyers.

This gave rise to new marketing tactics, like email, search engine optimization (SEO), and digital ads. Unfortunately, these tactics created a lot of noise. Inboxes were flooded with spam, articles were stuffed with barely relevant keywords to manipulate the search engine results pages (SERPs), and pop-ups cluttered websites.

Although regulation struggles to keep pace with technology, we've seen laws such as CAN-SPAM and GDPR seek to protect privacy, algorithm changes to improve content quality in SERPs, and disclosure requirements on advertising content.

We've also seen distribution move from rewarding organic content to pay-to-play models. Many marketers lament the pay-to-play model that is becoming more prevalent on social media sites and media outlets. This shift means that many brands are focusing on elevating individuals to increase the reach of their content, instead of investing more in pay-to-play outlets.

With the rise of AI-generated content, we're seeing further shifts in trust, marketing tactics, and platform responses. For example, Google announced its "Perspectives" tab, which aims to bring insights from real people into the SERPs.[8] It is no longer enough to optimize titles or keywords. Domain authority from the owner of an asset will no longer have the same impact that it once did. Google recognizes that people trust people like themselves, and they want to see real people sharing real experiences.

This is also why Google added an additional "E" to its previous content quality criteria. In 2023, it placed more importance on experience, rounding out the ranking criteria with the following elements:[9]

- **Experience:** Real-world or first-hand experience with the topic
- **Expertise:** Extensive formal training or real-world experience
- **Authoritativeness:** Certification or the ability to be seen as an authority on a given topic
- **Trustworthiness:** The overarching element that all of the above seek to satisfy.

This has practical implications for brands creating and distributing content. They can no longer rely solely on the strength of the brand or company name; they need to show the humans behind the screen.

This means including an actual name on bylines versus attributing content to the company or team. It means featuring practitioners in videos versus focusing only on executives or "official" company spokespeople. It means empowering employees and customers to speak in their own voices versus reading from a teleprompter with a script from the marketing or public relations department.

Presenting a real face and a real name can also de-escalate tense situations or bad experiences with a brand. It's often easy to argue with a faceless logo, hiding behind a screen. But when a human shows up? The tone changes.

These tactics sit at the intersection of several areas of the marketing mix: content (bylines), social media (personal handles), community (profile pictures and individual voices), events (going beyond slides), and product marketing (user feedback), to name a few. People trust people like themselves, so showing the humans is key to building that trust.

Many companies recognize this shift, giving rise to the need for "thought leadership." Unfortunately, too many teams mistake thought leadership for quality content or executive content. Thought leadership is not just content created by someone with a fancy title. It builds trust and credibility because it's built on deep expertise and experience. It articulates a strong and unique point of view. And it helps drive and shape the conversation, beyond a short-term sale.

It turns out that executives aren't always the best employees for thought leadership, in large part because they're so busy running the company that they can't or won't make time to codify their insights and participate in the larger conversation. Marketers need to broaden their lens as they search for subject-matter experts to elevate in the company in order to build trust with their audience. Remember, people trust people like themselves... and executives are only a small segment of potential customers, job candidates, partnerships, or investor base. Because people trust people like themselves, marketers need to partner with subject-matter experts at different levels of seniority and help them craft content that resonates with their peers.

In sum, we need to help our audience see themselves in content, products, and experiences created by people like themselves.

Trust and AI

The explosion of AI-generated content makes it more difficult to find and authenticate people we can trust. For example, despite Google's algorithm updates to improve search results, its AI search experiences also contribute to the problem of inaccurate or unhelpful information! In the spring of 2024, Google began including AI-generated summaries of search results. The promise was simple: Instead of forcing the searcher to sort through multiple web pages to find the answer they were looking for, Google would use AI to produce a summary of the relevant information, posted above all of the URLs in the search results. Unfortunately, the AI-generated summaries included patently absurd recommendations, like using glue to make cheese stickier on top of a pizza, or eating rocks to increase your daily mineral intake. While this advice is easily debunked by the average reader, potential for harm is much higher with lesser-known topics or less savvy users.

There have been cases of AI "hallucinating"—giving false facts about verifiable events, such as celebrity birthdays or historical events. People note that AI struggles with basic requests, for instance counting the number of letters in a word, or generating additional fingers and toes when creating images of people. While these examples sound humorous, the real-world implications of some AI-generated content are concerning. Without actual experts to verify the information, remove false or misleading claims, and generally ensure a standard of quality, it's much more difficult to know which information we can trust.

Unfortunately, merely slapping an expert's name on a piece of content to give it credibility is not new. This has been happening with human ghostwriters for years. Now, companies are trying to replace their content creators with AI asset generators and continuing to add a byline to make it seem like it came from an expert. No wonder audiences are skeptical of AI and its outputs!

Transparency is the key to combat this skepticism. Instead of hiding the fact that you used AI to write an article or generate an image, a clear statement about how you used AI helps build trust with the audience. Including a note that it was reviewed by a human, edited by a human, or vetted by a human helps the audience view the information as useful and credible. The issue is not necessarily that people use AI to create assets or answer questions; it's that the people (or the content) pretend to be something they're not. People want to know that you tested this theory, lived this experience, performed this work to solve a problem, or cited trustworthy sources if you haven't done it yourself.

In-person connections and live videos help to reinforce your overall trustworthiness, personal brand, and credibility, since it's more difficult to replicate these interactions with AI. It's getting more difficult to tell which content was written by AI, particularly if you're an expert at using AI tools and creating multi-step prompts or priming documents. Writing with a consistent style, voice, and tone that mirrors your in-person or video style helps to reinforce the credibility of your written content.

Laws and regulations are still quite far behind the technology, so AI providers and individuals are experimenting with how to build trust while using AI and incorporating AI into their offerings. Common disclosures include information about keeping user data private, details about how information loaded into an AI tool is stored and used, and security protocols when using AI.

Regardless of where you are in the AI adoption journey, it's essential to be explicit about how you're incorporating AI into your offerings, and when and how you include it as part of the audience journey.

REAL-WORLD EXAMPLE   Trust Insights—Built on Transparency

Trust Insights helps companies make better decisions with data. It uses machine learning, AI, automation, and analytics to help answer tough questions.

The company is all in on transparency. In fact, it's the first value listed on the website, which states, "We reject deception and secrecy. We are transparent and honest." Another core value reads, "We reject obfuscation and bull****. We are clear and direct."[10]

Co-founders Katie Robbert and Christopher Penn have been at the forefront of AI, and they're leading by example to build trust with AI. They include disclosures at the top of their personal and company content, noting how much of each asset was generated by AI, which tools and models they used, and how they used AI throughout the content. Their blog includes explicit callouts about content they've included as training data, noting that humans can skip past it.

In addition to the disclosures, the company shows its work with step-by-step images and explanations to ensure that the audience understands exactly how it gathers data, how it analyzes and transforms that data, how AI helps to accomplish these tasks, and how the outputs can be replicated by others. This explicit disclosure of AI usage helps to position Trust Insights as experts because it shows real-world case studies and challenges and builds trust with the audience by showing up exactly as it claims to be. In sum, it's trying to set the standard for transparency as AI becomes more mainstream.

The company transparency extends beyond AI-generated insights and content in a surprising way: it explicitly sells in one email newsletter per quarter! The subject line often reads, "Blatant Sales Pitch" or "Blatant Promo," and includes a note at the top that you can skip the email if you're not interested in buying anything. The email often includes the target audience in the first few lines, along with at least one core value proposition.

These emails are direct about who they're for, what they're selling, and why you should buy. There's no hidden agenda, no bait-and-switch content, and no false advertising. When you see the subject line, you know exactly what's coming.

That transparency builds trust! Readers feel confident subscribing to the newsletter and opening the other editions precisely because they know when Trust Insights is going to sell them something once per quarter.

Trust Insights remains true to its name, building trust through transparency in all touch-points. From the social posts shared by the co-founders, to disclosures about human-AI collaboration in the content, to the email subject lines; you know exactly who you're working with when you engage.

How to Build Trust and Rapport

Sonder (coined by John Koenig) has been called "the marketer's emotion." Koenig explains that sonder is:

> "the realization that each random passerby is living a life as vivid and complex as your own—populated with their own ambitions, friends, routines, worries, and inherited craziness—an epic story that continues invisibly around you like an anthill sprawling deep underground, with elaborate passageways to thousands of other lives that you'll never know existed, in which you might appear only once, as an extra sipping coffee in the background, as a blur of traffic passing on the highway, as a lighted window at dusk."[11]

Sonder shows understanding that audience members have their own hopes, users have their own dreams, customers have their own fears, and I, as a marketer, build the bridge. My role is to know and understand them and, hopefully, help them along the journey. In order to build such a bridge, marketers have to make the audience feel that the humans behind the brand are humans like themselves.

Consider the example of hand signals in various communities, such as the Jeep wave, the surfer shaka, and the motorcycle peace sign. These are signals of being part of the "in" group, knowing the language of the community, and acknowledging that "you're one of us." Members of each community feel a bond when someone flashes the hand sign because they know that this person is "like them", even though they might not know them personally. A signal like this means that we're not strangers. We can trust each other.

As marketers, we need to know, understand, and use signals to build trust, credibility, and rapport with our audience. We often talk about not using jargon, but shared signs and signals tell the audience that you know them. It's a way to show up and participate authentically, immersing yourself in the world where your audience lives.

Unfortunately, many marketers focus on short-term, transactional engagement, instead of immersion and connection. We often don't think of the audience as whole humans, but instead choose to focus on them as prospects, buyers, or users. We even use adversarial language as we talk about engaging with our audience:

- Hunt a prospect.
- Capture a lead.
- Lock down a contract.

But who wants to be hunted, captured, and locked down? No wonder our audience prefers to do their research in secret, without the "help" of a sales representative or company spokesperson!

Instead, we need to shift our thinking and our language to reflect the needs of our audience:

- Educate an audience.
- Help a customer.
- Delight a user.

Or better yet:

- Start a relationship.
- Maintain a relationship.
- Grow a relationship.

This starts with truly understanding the languages, habits, and needs of our audience, regardless of whether they purchase our offering to solve their problems.

- We must uncover the problem our audience actually faces.
- Not the problem we want to tell them about.
- Not the problem we solve.
- Not the problem we wish they had, so that we could swoop in with a solution.

The needs of our audience can change and evolve, which means that we, as marketers, need to go back to the audience again and again. The way to win and rewin their hearts, minds, and wallets is to create an open dialogue, become a trusted partner, and keep an open mind about how best to help them solve their problems.

But, it's not about asking our audience for information and time and favors. We need to embed ourselves in people's processes, forums, and use cases to understand how best to serve them. By giving individuals time to understand their audience, we can show up with solutions, instead of asking the audience to give us all the answers to make our lives easier.

REAL-WORLD EXAMPLE   Uber

When I was an undergraduate student studying marketing, I took a class about new product development. One of the groups pitched a carpool website that would match university students heading in the same direction.

The entire class pushed back on the idea:

- Who would get in a car with a stranger?
- How would you convince people it was safe?
- How would you guarantee that the person offering a ride was actually a student at the same university?

In short, how would you build enough trust among strangers for either party to be willing to get into a car and drive home together?

But Uber did just that. It convinced a bunch of strangers that riding together in a personal vehicle was a reasonable thing to do. How did they do it? By building and rebuilding trust, over and over again.

Uber launched in 2009 and has since climbed to over a $150 billion valuation in 2024. It has faced significant ups and downs, including scandals involving sexual harassment, clashes with regulators, and employee relations issues. Yet, drivers keep driving, and riders keep riding.

In 2017, Uber faced significant hurdles, and hired trust expert and Harvard Business School professor Frances Frei to help improve the company's reputation. Frei recounts her time working with Uber leadership in a TED podcast, detailing three key markers of trust: logic, authenticity, and empathy.[12]

- **Logic** is the belief that your reasoning and judgment are sound.
- **Authenticity** is the belief that someone experiences the real you.
- **Empathy** is the belief that you care about me and my success.

Together, they found that Uber had an empathy problem, particularly with drivers. The company had already addressed some of the key trust concerns for riders by adding functionality including real-time route tracking to ensure a driver was actually heading towards the intended destination, sharing details about personal and vehicle screenings required to become a driver, and the ability to share trip details with trusted contacts. Each of these features focused on building rider trust, with the individual drivers and Uber as a brand, mediating the transaction.

But, trust among drivers had degraded. Frances Frei discovered that one particular element, empathy, was at an all-time low. Drivers felt that Uber had the ability to be empathetic, but wasn't using it with drivers. One concrete example was sending drivers in the opposite direction of their home, even though they had marked their last ride for the night. Drivers felt that Uber was not invested in their success. The company had tilted so far in favor of riders that it was ignoring the needs of a key constituent: the drivers. Frei diagnosed this core breakdown in trust and worked with the Uber leadership to implement changes to restore trust by improving empathy.

As we've seen over and over, trust is not just about platitudes or fluffy feelings. It's about action, commitment, and consistency. In Uber's case, it added tipping for drivers, made changes to the "last ride," and gave them an outlet for more speedy responses to concerns and complaints. Uber aimed to show the drivers that it cared about them and was invested in their success.

Introducing Human-Centered Marketing

As we've seen, humans solving problems for humans is key to building trust and driving business outcomes. Throughout the rest of this book, we'll dive into details about the pitfalls of the traditional approach to marketing, evolving practices to increase awareness and conversion, and how to truly build trust and rapport with your audience.

First, a disclaimer: I wrote every word of this book with my own two hands. A human editor helped me hone each chapter, using her own expertise. A human designer worked on the cover and formatting for all the images.

No artificial intelligence, no ghostwriters, no piecing together work from unknown sources. Just a group of humans with formal education in our respective fields, years of lived experience, and expertise derived from solving problems multiple times. I developed my frameworks in response to answering questions for my own marketing teams, wrestling with the day-to-day challenges that my colleagues and I faced, and through conversations with fellow practitioners.

I hope this assurance helps you trust the information in this book, knowing that I've tested the frameworks myself. I failed, iterated, and improved over time, and codified my experiences and the experiences of my peers to help you improve your approach to marketing.

After all, humans trust humans like themselves. And I'm just like you; a marketer who wants to meet the needs of my audience, hit my business goals, and, hopefully, have a little fun along the way.

Second, a promise: You'll walk away with actionable frameworks and tactics that you can implement today. I aim to make it simple for you to evolve your approach to marketing. (See Figure 1.1.)

Figure 1.1   Human-Centered Marketing Frameworks

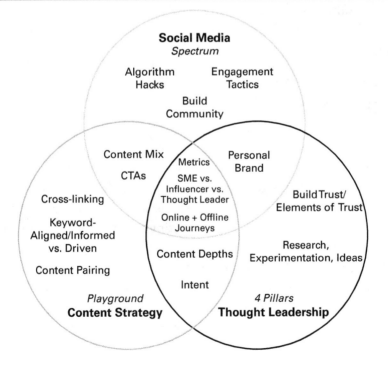

We'll start by rethinking the traditional linear funnel. We know that buyers have never traveled a linear path to a purchase, but we've continued to use the old framework because we haven't had a replacement. I introduce the *playground framework* as a way to map the audience journey more accurately, with tactics including content depths, intent, and time horizons to help you create a content and distribution strategy to meet your audience where they are, no matter which path they take.

Then, we'll discuss how social media has changed, using the *social media spectrum* to understand how to move from communication, to conversation, to community. Using real-world examples, you'll learn the new rules of social media to connect with your audience, build rapport, and, ultimately, drive value.

Last, I'll share the *four pillars of thought leadership*. Thought leadership helps your audience think in a new way and take action in a new direction. It goes beyond quality content or contrarian thinking, and codifies new tactics, strategy, and visions to enable your audience to move into the future. Building thought leaders with high credibility, a well-known profile, a prolific publishing cadence, and strong depth of ideas helps the brand build long-term trust with a variety of audiences.

Conclusion

Marketing has long claimed to be about people. It's what attracted me to the profession in the first place. But as technology advanced, we shifted our focus to efficiency by automating content creation, return on investment, attribution by insisting we track every touchpoint, and growth at any cost by insisting that every tactic must scale indefinitely.

We need to get back to the foundations of humans showing how their offering solves problems for humans. I hope that when you finish this book, you'll feel inspired and equipped to achieve your goals by getting back to human-centered marketing.

Chapter Summary

- Trust has been declining since 2005, particularly among publishing outlets and those with traditional markers of authority, such as a leadership role in a business or a government position.

- People trust people likes themselves, and having a personal experience or relationship with leaders and peers increases trust.

- People buy from people and businesses they trust, so, building trust with your audience drives real business impact, including purchases, job applications, and institutional investment.

- Marketers need to focus on building trust and rapport with their audience, taking a human-centered approach to the audience journey, instead of focusing on the traditional linear funnel, outdated social media practices, and thin content in place of true thought leadership.

Notes

1 Ries, T.E., et al (2018) *2018 Edelman Trust Barometer Global Report*, Edelman, edelman.com/sites/g/files/aatuss191/files/2018-10/2018_ Edelman_Trust_Barometer_Global_Report_FEB.pdf (archived at https://perma.cc/D865-BE5N)

2 Ries, T.E., et al (2019) *2019 Edelman Trust Barometer Global Report*, Edelman, edelman.com/sites/g/files/aatuss191/files/2019-03/2019_ Edelman_Trust_Barometer_Global_Report.pdf? (archived at https://perma.cc/9SYR-SEBQ)

3 Ries, T.E., et al (2020–2024) Edelman Trust Barometer, Edelman, edelman.com/trust/trust-barometer (archived at https://perma.cc/ J6TB-8VRL)

4 Ries, T.E., et al (2023) *2023 Edelman Trust Barometer Global Report*, Edelman, edelman.com/sites/g/files/aatuss191/files/2023-03/2023%20 Edelman%20Trust%20Barometer%20Global%20Report%20FINAL. pdf (archived at https://perma.cc/Z76J-JFYF)

5 Ries, T.E., et al (2024) *2024 Edelman Trust Barometer Global Report*, Edelman, edelman.com/sites/g/files/aatuss191/files/2024-02/2024%20 Edelman%20Trust%20Barometer%20Global%20Report_FINAL.pdf (archived at https://perma.cc/W2KT-SWDZ)

6 Ries, T.E., et al (2022) *2022 Edelman Trust Barometer Global Report*, Edelman, edelman.com/sites/g/files/aatuss191/files/2022-01/2022%20 Edelman%20Trust%20Barometer%20FINAL_Jan25.pdf (archived at https://perma.cc/LB3V-3BBP)

7 Edelman, R. (2005) *Edelman Trust Barometer 2005: The Sixth Global Opinion Leaders Study*, Edelman, edelman.com/sites/g/files/aatuss191/ files/2018-10/2005-Edelman-Trust-Barometer-Global-Findings.pdf (archived at https://perma.cc/5HT9-QGAS)

8 Clark, L. (2023) Learn From Others' Experiences with More Perspective on Search, Google blog, *The Keyword*, May 23, blog. google/products/search/google-search-perspectives (archived at https://perma.cc/TRF4-ZUH3)

9 Tucker, E. (2022) Our Latest Update to the Quality Rater Guidelines: E-A-T Gets an Extra E for Experience, Google Search Central Blog, December 15, developers.google.com/search/blog/2022/12/google-raters-guidelines-e-e-a-t (archived at https://perma.cc/X85D-JLGF)

10 Penn, C. and Robbert, K. (2023) About Trust Insights: Our Values, Trust Insights, trustinsights.ai/about/what-we-stand-for (archived at https://perma.cc/QB63-2JJA)

11 Koenig, John (2012) Sonder, *The Dictionary of Obscure Sorrows*, www.dictionaryofobscuresorrows.com/post/23536922667/sonder (archived at https://perma.cc/K4P9-LQBK)

12 Frei, F. and Morriss, A. (2023) Uber, and How to Fix Things when Trust is Broken, *Fixable* podcast series, August 28, ted.com/podcasts/ fixable/uber-and-how-to-fix-things-when-trust-is-broken-transcript (archived at https://perma.cc/B2EY-X5J8)

Content Strategy: The Right Message to the Right People

02

The Funnel is Dead. Use a Playground Instead

Mapping content to the traditional funnel adds no value, since the journey behaves more like a playground than a linear progression. Pitfalls of the traditional funnel include assuming that every person in the audience intends to and will become a customer, underestimating the sophistication of the buyer, and offering limited options for post-purchase retention strategies.

As discussed in the previous chapter, building a seamless, delightful journey on a foundation of trust means that we must fundamentally rethink our framework for the audience journey. Most marketers are familiar with the traditional funnel to outline the buyer's journey, focusing on three key phases: awareness, consideration, and decision. The funnel assumes that the audience journey begins with awareness, when, in fact, the audience journey begins long before marketers recognize that this person is on a journey.

Newer iterations of the funnel attempt to acknowledge this by differentiating between "problem aware," "solution aware," and "offering aware," with problems, solutions, and offerings noted at each later phase. Newer models also include additional phases to account for the rise of subscription offerings, including retention, cross-sell, up-sell, and advocacy. However, these phases often result in a looping decision journey, forcing people back into a rudimentary awareness phase.

As I wrestled with this problem, I decided that we need a new model. And I thought I solved it: a jungle gym. Unfortunately, it also falls short, as there's really only one objective, which is reaching the top of the gym. That's still me as a marketer forcing my audience to go on a journey that I want them to go on, reaching an objective that *I* set, as quickly as possible.

At their core, traditional models use a company-centric lens to simplify a journey that leads to a purchase. They fail to recognize that the audience is broader than those who are ready, willing, and able to make a purchase.

Consider the first phase, "awareness." Awareness of what? The problem your company solves? The offering your company sells? The features of your product or capabilities of your service? Even the concept of "the buyer's journey" implies that buying is the only goal. The exchange of value is heavily weighted in favor of the company, and marketers focus only on extracting that value from the audience. It's seen as a one-way journey from becoming aware of the company and its offering, consideration of a few companies and offerings, to, ultimately, purchasing an offering. Then the journey ends from a marketing perspective, and it's on to hunting down the next round of prospects to funnel to a purchase.

Introducing the Playground

Instead, we need to think about the journey as a playground: people can go up, down, sideways, and around. They can go in any order. They can enter and exit as they please. And they can use content in the "wrong" way.

For example, pricing is traditionally considered a "bottom of funnel" conversation. I experienced the pain of being forced into the funnel when my manager tasked me with purchasing new software. During the quarterly planning process, I needed to request budget, but I didn't know how much to ask for. So, I started searching around for the big players in the space. I attempted to find pricing on their websites, trying to avoid scheduling a sales call, as I was just starting to make the case to ask for budget. Unfortunately, most companies obscured their pricing, filling their pages with calls to action, such as "Contact Sales," "Book a demo," or "Learn more." I ended up filling out several "contact sales" forms, asking for ballpark pricing for a range of licenses and service levels. Most of the responses insisted that I book a formal meeting to have a conversation. I managed to get one rep to give me pricing without scheduling a meeting, and I used that estimate to secure budget for a tool to solve my problem.

After securing budget, I sent a note back to the providers that met our criteria, asking to book a demo. I outlined our problem set, timeline for choosing a solution, and key capabilities that we needed. And yet, most reps opened our calls with multiple slides trying to convince me that this problem was important, the costs of ignoring it, and ultimately, trying to convince me that I should prioritize the problem. But I had already bought in on the problem! And I had bought in on purchasing a tool in their category to solve the problem. And I had a budget and a solid idea of key features I needed in a solution. By the time I attended the "top of funnel" call, I was already in the consideration or purchase phase. Still, the reps insisted that I go through each phase of the funnel. They couldn't adapt their scripts to the journey I was actually taking.

How many times do you force your audience to go through unnecessary steps because you're trying to make them buy when they're not ready, or, worse, you add friction to the buying process because you need to check the boxes on providing a white paper and a demo and a case study?

Why does this happen? It stems from the idea that we need to push prospects down the funnel to become leads and keep moving them through until they become customers.

Pitfalls of the Customer Journey Map

Consider a typical customer journey map (Figure 2.1). Again, the name "customer journey map" implies that these people will become customers.

Figure 2.1 Linear Customer Journey

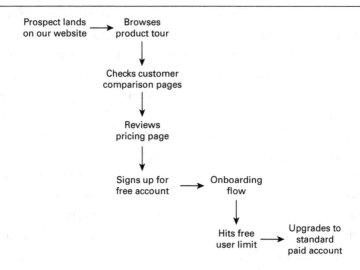

This sample customer journey map for a software-as-a-service (SaaS) company assumes a "prospect" moves along a linear process to eventually become a paying customer.

The assumptions begin with the first step in the journey. For example, a typical customer journey map often starts with actions such as "Prospect lands on our website" or "Prospect searches for a solution to a problem." Some marketers try to take a step back and start with "Prospect faces a problem, and decides they need a solution." But how do we know they're a prospect? Where were they before they landed on the website?

From there, the journey traverses owned properties that are easy to measure. The prospect clicks on the page about your offering. Then they read a customer case study, linked from the offering page. Then they review the pricing page. Then they sign up or start a free trial or contact sales. Done!

We've effectively mapped the customer journey from "awareness" when they land on the website, to "consideration" when they explore the offering, case study, and pricing pages, and "decision" when they sign up or contact sales. We can see every touchpoint because our attribution software makes it easy to track, as long as someone stays on our website or clicks on our newsletter link or spends time in our community forum.

Ultimately, every customer journey map ends with the prospect becoming a lead and deciding to purchase the company's offering. This linear journey map ignores retention, cross-sell, up-sell, and expansion opportunities. While the looping journey does at least acknowledge the additional post-purchase phase, it fails to capture the complexity. For example, many software-as-a-service companies have user limits for different tiers of their product offerings. With the rise of product-led growth (PLG) as a key go-to-market motion, many SaaS products include a free tier, with user gates, feature gates, or both, to prompt free users to become paying customers. Traditional journey maps obscure the messy middle of the customer journey, with weird hacks to stay under the user limit, lengthy negotiations on larger contracts for seat expansion, and fighting competitors when it is time for the customer to renew. We simply note that some customers churned, some stayed at the same spending level, and some accounts grew.

This highlights another pitfall of the funnel and associated journey maps to move people through the funnel. It's a retrospective measurement tool, not a forward-looking strategy tool.

If you map the journeys of people who did, in fact, become customers, then you are correct in starting with a prospect having a problem, searching for a solution, and ultimately, choosing your offering. If, however, you are trying to build a net-new audience, hone your narratives to resonate with that audience, and map your content and distribution strategy, you can't simply look at what happened in the past, on owned platforms, in the condensed time period where the buying process "officially" started. In addition, consider a post-purchase scenario where the marketer makes the journey more difficult for a customer precisely because they want to track the interaction in more detail. Collecting more information gives us a false sense of security. If we know just a bit more about this person, surely we can convince them to spend more money.

Meanwhile, our need to track every interaction and map it to an up-sell or cross-sell or renewal means that we alienate our existing customers. For example, many SaaS products can include messages in their products for customers to see. When a new feature is released, it might trigger a notification that pops up to alert the user. Similar messages can be used to announce pricing updates, account upgrades, or trial expiration notices, or other content the company deems relevant, like webinars or conferences. But users often view this content as advertising. They don't necessarily differentiate between an announcement for a potentially helpful new feature, a notification meant to sell them an upgraded subscription, or an invitation to a free, informative event.

Worse still, the experience is often poor if the user clicks on the pop-up. Let's say they click on a notification to watch a webinar. Presumably, we already know who this person is, since they've just followed up on a notification from their account in our product, but we bring them to a landing page with a lengthy registration form for the webinar. We ask them to, manually, fill out the required form, giving us their first name, last name, email address, title, company name, company size, annual revenue, and which products they're interested in hearing about or already using. But, don't we already have this information? The customer came to this page from within their product account. They already gave us their name and company information to sign up for an account.

We've put our need for easy tracking, journey mapping, and data collection above the customer experience.

This is taken even further if we ask for data that we won't use, such as a physical address or phone number. What action, exactly, do we plan to take with that information? Do we intend to call the customer? Are we planning to mail them something? It might appear that having more information about our users and customers will allow us to personalize their journeys or understand their pain-points more deeply, but putting these obstacles in the way actually makes their journey more difficult.

Traditional funnel models also fail to recognize the differences between a user and an economic buyer. Many marketers recognize that buying involves multiple different people, but they assume that each stakeholder joins the process in a linear way. For example, in larger companies, an economic buyer might need to go through a procurement process that includes a security assessment, compliance checklist, and legal or contract review before bringing in a new tool. The linear funnel assumes that these stakeholders need to be addressed in the "decision" phase of the buying process. And yet, ask anyone who's been through procurement in a large enterprise, and they'll tell you that it's difficult, and, often, a deterrent to even starting a buying process. In order to convince me to buy, you need to convince me that I'll be able to buy. If you make it easy for me to make it through the procurement process, I'm much more likely to choose you as a vendor because I know that I'll be successful in completing the process.

Consider another scenario, where individual teams are empowered to purchase tools and services on their own. These teams are all in the "post-purchase" phase. At some point, the invoices might be large enough to warrant consolidation, which might trigger a wider vendor review. In that case, you've won over many users, but the economic buyer is now in the "awareness" phase, as they've just discovered you as a vendor. Or, they might need to be convinced that solving this problem should continue to be a priority at all. Alternatively, the buyers might immediately move to the "consideration" phase by opening a request for proposal (RFP) or researching competitors. Maybe they've bought in on the problem, but they want to explore different solutions. They might need to learn about different possible solutions, even though there's already a vendor solving this problem.

Once you decide to consolidate a contract, the spend might be big enough to require a more thorough vetting by the procurement, security, compliance, and legal teams. At this point, who knows which phase of the funnel you're in? Is it "retention" with the users, who no longer actually have buying power? Is it awareness or consideration with the economic buyer? Is it awareness or decision with teams who have the ability to block the deal, but aren't the economic buyer?

As you can see, attempting to map content to a linear funnel by also mapping linear personas becomes quite a challenge!

These scenarios also minimize or ignore the sophistication of the buyer. In a B2B (business-to-business) context, most buyers are quite sophisticated. They're well-versed in the problem space, and might have purchased solutions in the past. They're equipped to do their own research, and often prefer working through the initial vetting phases before reaching out to a company to initiate a buying process.

In fact, TrustRadius found that, in 2021, 43 percent of buyers reported consulting with vendor representatives, and that number dropped to an average of one out of four buyers in all but the largest deal sizes. Instead, buyers preferred to conduct their own research, with a bias towards non-vendor-provided material. Buyers favored free trials or accounts (56 per cent), user reviews (55 per cent), and community forums (37 per cent) over vendor-provided materials such as customer references (15 per cent), blogs (14 per cent), and marketing collateral (14 per cent).[1]

This trend continued in a 2024 report from 6sense, a company that arms revenue teams with data to accelerate deal conversions. It found that, when B2B buyers directly engage sellers, they are already 70 per cent through their buying process.[2]

We see over and over that by the time a marketer becomes aware that someone is in the buying process, they're significantly behind the buyer's knowledge of the problem space, research into the solution space, and affinity for a select list of solution providers. They're not coming to the company website cold, or blindly reaching out to a salesperson. Instead, they've consulted a curated list of trusted sources, including conversations with their personal network, crowd-sourced information, and recommendations from peers on social media and forums, and they've read about the pros and cons of different providers from people like themselves.

Go-To-Market and Content Strategy Foundations

In order to deliver the right message to the right person, we need to build the journey like a playground. We can't map content to the traditional funnel. So, how *do* we map content? In the next chapter, we'll discuss details of how to map content with depths, intent, and time horizons. However, before we start, we need a solid, overarching content strategy that aligns with the overall go-to-market (GTM) motions at the company.

First, you need to understand which GTM motion(s) you're using. You can refer to the motions outlined by GTM partners, which include inbound, outbound, product, event, partner, and community.[3] Alternatively, you can reference broader motions, such as sales-led, enterprise, and self-serve or flywheel motions. Your company may use more than one motion, which might mean that you have multiple content strategies to address key elements within each motion.

In a PLG company, for example, core elements of the GTM motion include removing friction from the buying process and allowing the audience to self-serve for initial product adoption, seeing the benefits of upgrading and paying more for the product via feature gates or user limits. The overarching content strategy includes sharing content that helps the audience adopt and use the products (such as templates, guides, and short tutorials or demo videos) as a way of removing friction throughout the product exploration, purchase, and retention stages of the buyer's journey. This GTM motion tends to include organic content and search engine optimization (SEO) as key elements of the overarching content strategy, with metrics like entrances and free account sign-ups.

In contrast, companies focused on enterprise or sales-led motions have an overarching content strategy that is more targeted, focusing more on one-to-one or one-to-few assets and channels. They rely more heavily on content for sales enablement (such as battle-cards against competitors, pitch decks, and datasheets), analyst reports, thought leadership, and account-based marketing (ABM) programs, with metrics like marketing-qualified leads (MQLs) and a marketing-influenced pipeline.

SNAPSHOT OF DIFFERENCES BETWEEN PLG AND SALES-LED MOTIONS

Product-led growth and sales-led growth are two of the most popular GTM motions. Many companies choose to start with one or the other, but technology companies tend to adopt both over time. Table 2.1 presents a summary of key differences in channels and tactics between the two motions.

Table 2.1   PLG Activities Versus Sales-Led Activities

PLG Activities	Sales-Led Activities
Copywriting	Messaging
Search engine optimization	Sales enablement
Competitive comparison pages	Battle-cards
Digital campaigns (generally focused on building awareness among audiences who are unlikely to be in the market in the short term)	Sales campaigns (generally focused on closing short-term, in-market buyers)
Community evangelists	Analyst firms
Review sites (e.g. G2, Capterra, Trustpilot)	Analyst reports (e.g. Gartner Magic Quadrant, Forrester Wave)
Forums and social media	Executive briefings and customer advisory boards
Point products or project-based fees	Solutions or retainers

Both GTM motions include other elements of the marketing mix, such as brand-building, communications and press, field marketing or events, and analytics. If you add a GTM motion or use multiple motions, you'll need to adapt your strategy to incorporate relevant assets, channels, and tactics.

Once you identify your key motions, it's time to build out your content strategy. As noted, you might need multiple content approaches if you're using several GTM motions. Your content strategy should address key issues including:

- information about your audience—their needs, pain-points, and existing knowledge about the problem and solution space
- business goals, both short and long term, in alignment with the GTM motion(s)
- key messages for the brand and each of the company offerings.

The content strategy should be broader than just an editorial calendar, a single asset type, or a single distribution channel. It should also include key teams, processes, and tools to create, share, and measure your content consistently. I recommend bringing multiple teams together to collaborate on your content strategy.

Depending on the size of your company, you might include the following specialists to answer specific questions in order to create the content strategy.

Product marketing: Who are we talking to, and what are we talking about?

- Who is our audience? Product marketers are responsible for understanding the target audience, ideal customer profile (ICP), and influential personas in the buyer's journey. They should bring questions that the audience might be asking, identify gaps in information that currently exists, and give insights about pain-points that we need to address.
- What is our message? Product marketers are also responsible for shaping how we talk about our solution, with differentiated messaging and positioning against competitors, as well as value propositions and proof-points to help the audience decide to buy and use our offering.

Analyst relations, communications, and SEO teams: What is the market talking about?

- What trends are shaping the industry? Analyst relations teams work with analyst firms to understand the overarching industry trends and vendor requirements for each category. Analysts help define the problem space and shape the criteria that the audience might use when evaluating potential solutions.

- What news and information are timely for the media and influencers? The communications and/or public relations teams keep a pulse on which topics, trends, and news are top of mind for journalists, news outlets, and other media, including popular podcasts, blogs, and social media accounts.

- Which topics, keywords, and formats are performing well in search engine results pages (SERPs)? Larger companies often include a separate SEO team, but people with this background might also sit in a content marketing or editorial team. They understand how search engine algorithms are changing, how the audience is searching for information, and which language the audience uses when searching for problems and solutions in your category.

Performance and demand-generation: Where are we talking, and how do we reach people?

- Where does the audience spend time? Performance marketers and demand-generation teams focus on the channels where the audience spends time, consumes information, and makes purchases. They help find new channels and new audiences within those channels.

- Which channels and assets help us reach our goals? These experts also help us understand which channels are performing well, based on relevant metrics throughout the audience journey. They also bring data to show which assets perform best in each channel, with a focus on paid and owned channels.

Content marketing: How are we talking, and how do we connect the journey?

- What are the core topics, themes, and narratives? Content marketers help teams go beyond features and competitor comparisons. They help teams address the problem space, solution space, and practices required to help the audience eliminate their pain-points. They think about which narratives are best suited for different assets, which assets are best suited for different channels, and they create content for use throughout the journey.

- Which asset types and content formats should we include? Not all narratives make sense for each asset, and some asset types and formats might not be effective for the company. Content marketers use their narrative expertise and content creation skills to match narratives with asset types and formats to fuel the campaigns and paid channels.

- How do we match our narratives and asset types to different channels? In larger companies, content marketers help drive strategy for organic channels, including adapting and repurposing content, and they partner with teammates in performance marketing and demand-generation to ensure assets are performing well in relevant channels.

Additional teams

- **Brand:** If you do not already have brand guidelines for your core values, voice and tone, and visual identity, you should include the brand team in the content strategy planning sessions.

- **Customer-facing teams:** You might also bring in sales representatives and team members from customer success, solution engineering, or other customer-facing teams to provide more insight into the audience and their needs. Subject-matter experts from the product or solution teams might also be included to talk about key areas of differentiation in the offering.

- **Operations and/or program managers:** These ensure that all teams have visibility and tracking for all content and distribution programs. They often set up processes and templates to help each team obtain the necessary stakeholder buy-in, feedback, and approvals.

An effective content strategy includes the following foundational elements:

- **Audience:** Who is our audience?
- **Market:** How are we differentiated in the market? This includes our offering, messaging, and key value propositions.
- **Outcomes:** What outcomes are we trying to drive? What are our goals, and how are we measuring progress towards these goals? What are our key performance indicators and metrics to prove that we're hitting our goals?

- **Content pillars and narratives:** What are the core topics, themes, and unique angle addressed in our content to help acquire, convert, retain, and grow our customer base?

- **Channels:** Where does our audience spend time? Which channels perform best for each metric and outcome? Which channels are essential as opposed to experimental? What is the channel mix for the year?

These foundational elements and team structures should not change frequently if the company is more mature. If the company is in a high-growth phase, it might expand the teams and divide the responsibilities. If there's a change in the market dynamics or the company adds a new audience segment to its market, it will need to revisit its messaging and core narratives. If there's a significant change in the solution offerings, it might make sense to consider shifting or adding a new GTM motion, which might result in new content needs and goals. This is common for companies who, for example, start with a PLG motion and later decide they want to sell to enterprise buyers and increase their average contract value. They build out a sales team and incorporate more of the tactics, touchpoints, and content noted in the sales-led motion.

However, these strategic decisions should not shift without a good reason. Continually changing the focus from one audience to another, updating the messaging and positioning based on the whims of internal stakeholders, and creating assets for the sake of chasing new trends will result in confusion in the market, inefficient creation and distribution, and frustrated teams.

Conclusion

As marketers, we need to think holistically about the journey, making it seamless and delightful. It's no longer about rushing people to a purchase via as few touchpoints as possible; it's about allowing them to choose their own path in a way that helps them reach their destination.

Yes, we need to sell products. In subscription model businesses, we need to win and rewin the hearts, minds, and wallets of our audiences. That means we need to enable them to use the products and show the value of the products to the decision-makers. This means we need to rethink how to create content strategy, execute assets, and measure the journey.

Chapter Summary

- Traditional funnel models do not represent the modern buyer's journey.
- Audiences prefer to do the majority of their research without engaging with a salesperson.
- Marketers need to treat the individual's journey like a playground, allowing them to go up, down, and sideways.
- The goal is no longer to rush people into a purchase with as few touchpoints as possible, but rather to create a journey with seamless handoffs, helpful content, and frictionless buying options.

Notes

1 TrustRadius (2022) *2022 Buying Disconnect: The Age of the Self-Serve Buyer*, go.trustradius.com/rs/827-FOI-687/images/TrustRadius_2022_ B2B_Buying_Disconnect_6.27.22.pdf (archived at https://perma.cc/ TG6X-UU8T)

2 6sense Research (2023) *Out of Sight, Almost Out of Time: The 2023 6sense B2B Buyer Experience Report*, 6sense, 6sense.com/report/ buyer-experience (archived at https://perma.cc/XJ3Z-ULJ4)

3 GTM Partners (2023) *The 6 Go-To-Market Motions*, hub.gtmpartners. com/gtm-research-guidance/the-7-go-to-market-motions (archived at https://perma.cc/BCN3-L3YJ)

Elements of the Playground

03

Content Depths, Intent, and Time Horizon

In order to create a smart, seamless, and impactful journey that resembles a playground, marketers need to move away from mapping content to a traditional linear funnel or looping decision journey. Instead, they should use content depths, intent, and time horizons to inform their content strategy.

In the previous chapter, we discussed moving on from the funnel to the playground because the traditional linear funnel does not represent the audience journey, and even more progressive models, such as the looping decision journey or customer journey maps, still force the audience into a journey that ends in a purchase, based on marketing touchpoints.

Instead, we need to imagine the journey as a playground, allowing the audience to go up, down, and sideways, to enter and exit as they please, and to use content the "wrong" way. Marketers need to be smart enough to create a seamless and delightful journey, no matter which path their audience takes.

We also need to balance limited time, budget, and human resources to make sure we're maximizing our opportunities. We can't create every asset, and we can't appear in every channel. We need to think strategically about which narratives resonate most, which asset types are best for each narrative, and which channels to prioritize to reach our audience. To do this, we'll use three models to map our content and consider each asset available during the journey:

- content depth

- intent
- time horizon.

Building Your Narrative with Content Depths

Many companies start with the information they want their audience to know: We're launching a new product, we've released a new feature, we're offering a discount, and so on. Instead, marketers need to go back to the information the audience wants to consume. This means that marketers should focus more on narrative development than feature lists. Narratives should have enough depth to fuel content across multiple angles, asset types, distribution channels, and audience intents.

As you think about narrative topics, keep it channel- and deliverable-agnostic for now. Start with big themes that you want to cover, regardless of whether you're writing an article, creating a video, or standing on a stage. These themes should overlap with the wants and needs of your audience.

DEFINING CONTENT DEPTHS

You need to be able to address the topic at all three depths: conceptual, strategic, and tactical.

- **Conceptual:** These are the overarching themes, and should be limited to three to five core ideas. These are theoretical and philosophical in nature, with a much more abstract application. These ideas form the foundation on which to build strategic and tactical ideas. When creating content at this level, don't be too concerned about the "how." Instead, focus on the "what" and the "why" of the idea. This content helps the audience think about the problem space. The conceptual level focuses on high-level and aspirational outcomes. If there's measurement available, that's great, but at this level, it's unlikely.

- **Strategic:** This level focuses on the process, tools, and key knowledge components that must be included to make the conceptual ideas a reality. This level should enable tangible outcomes that can be measured in the long run and help the audience think about the solution space. The content equips the audience to conduct their own research, gives them frameworks and criteria for success, and helps them envision the impact that conceptual ideas can have in their organization.

- **Tactical:** This is the nitty-gritty "how" level, where the rubber meets the road. If you want to achieve the high-level outcomes of the conceptual level, and you've put in place the processes and tools at the strategic level, what are the daily tasks, habits, and conversations that need to happen? This content should be prescriptive in nature, and offer step-by-step instructions, links to specific exercises, and detailed templates or worksheets to help the audience implement the conceptual and strategic ideas. This level can include short-term metrics and outcomes.

In general, we should focus on no more than five conceptual ideas, though three is better to ensure the content is connected. Practically, this means that we likely align the conceptual ideas with larger programs or campaigns for each market, offering, or product portfolio. We can then map five to seven strategic ideas to each concept, and create tactical content on an ongoing basis. The strategic examples can be shared among the conceptual ideas, and tactics can be duplicated across multiple strategies and concepts. These can change over time, and we might address a topic from multiple angles to achieve different depths. Note that these are ideas for each depth, *not* assets or channels or angles.

In general, we want the conceptual ideas to be valid for at least 18 to 24 months and the strategic ideas to be valid for at least 12 to 18 months. Tactics can be valid for much shorter periods, and tactics can change as we learn more information, follow market trends, and/or address competitive threats.

When I share content depths, people often confuse the three content depths for the three phases in a traditional linear funnel. However, these do not map one to one: Conceptual does not mean top of funnel, strategic does not mean middle of funnel, and tactical does not mean bottom of funnel. This makes sense if you review the definitions of each element:

- The awareness stage of the linear funnel is commonly defined as the time the prospect becomes aware of the company and its offering. In contrast, **conceptual depth** refers to the what and why of an idea and defining the general problem space.

- The consideration stage of the linear funnel is commonly defined as the time when the prospect is evaluating solutions and debating whether to purchase a solution from a vendor, and which solution to buy. In contrast, **strategic depth** is about processes, key knowledge components, and, potentially, the general tooling landscape.

- The decision stage of the linear funnel is commonly defined as the point at which the prospect chooses a solution and vendor, or chooses not to make a purchase at all. In contrast, **tactical depth** includes prescriptive steps and ongoing actions that someone takes.

Let's look at some general examples. First, consider a user on a free tier of a product. This person is already well aware of the company and their offering and, in fact, they're using the product in their day-to-day job. But, they haven't purchased. Thus, a tutorial showing them how to use a new feature might be quite useful for them. This might be considered *tactical* content depth, since it gives step-by-step instructions. But, if the user is not ready, willing, or able to make a purchase, then it can't be considered bottom of funnel, which usually means that someone is at the purchase stage.

Similarly, content that focuses on practices or processes, regardless of product use, can be mapped to the *strategic* content depth, but not the middle of funnel, since middle of funnel means that the person is considering whether to make a purchase. For example, think about an attribution software provider, like Dreamdata. It shares content about choosing an attribution model, noting the benefits and pitfalls of popular models, such as first-touch attribution, last-touch attribution, and multi-touch attribution. Choosing an attribution model is indicative of what the marketing organization values, and a decision that must be made, regardless of whether you purchase or currently use the Dreamdata product.

As you can see, the definitions of content depths are not at all the same as the definitions of the linear funnel.

Intent-Based Content

Content needs to be based on the intent and immediate next action for the *audience*. There's a misconception that the "best" content is "educational" content. Unfortunately, this means that content creators twist the meaning to insist that *any* content is "learning" content. For example:

- The product tour teaches people about our features, therefore it's educational.
- This tutorial teaches people how to use a feature, so it's educational.
- This eBook teaches people about why our cloud products are more secure than on-premises products...

In fact, we see that the actual intent of each of these statements is *buying*, *using*, and *trusting*, respectively.

We can shift our mindset to understand the true, underlying intent by thinking about the immediate next action:

- Do we want them to sign up?
- Upgrade?
- Log in?
- Fix a problem?

All of these actions represent non-learning-focused outcomes.

Definitions of Key Intents

- **Trust intent:** Content that generally builds a sense of trust and affinity at a high level.

- **Buy intent**: Any content that pushes the person to take action to access our products or services. This could be a free sign-up, a trial for an upgrade edition, an invitation that expands the number of users, or upgrading to a paid edition in a product-focused company. This could be an initial consultation or discovery call, free estimate, or pilot project in a services-focused company. If it's meant to get people closer to paying the company money, it's buy-intent content.

- **Use intent**: Any content that pushes the person to take action in the product or engage in the services. It could be alerting them to a new free feature, suggesting a free integration, or demos/tutorial/onboarding information to enable them to use the products. It could be attending the weekly office hours, reviewing the monthly report, or bringing an advisor onsite for a quarterly workshop. If it's meant to help the customer extract value from the solution they purchased, it's use-intent content.

- **Help intent** (remediation intent): Any content that enables the user to troubleshoot a problem. It answers prompts such as, "Why isn't (this feature) working?" or "I can't access (the account)". This content is closely related to use-intent content, but tends to be accessed less frequently and only when there's a problem implementing the solution.

- **Learn intent**: True learn-intent content only requires the consumer to think about what they've consumed. They don't need to make a payment. They don't need to log in. They don't need to present a case to their stakeholders. They might share on social media, they might reflect, or they might implement a new practice that doesn't require any additional tools or access.

Using Intent-Based Content in the Playground

A common conversation among marketers seems to imply that any content that sells is wrong, negative, or otherwise not serving the audience.

I disagree. If someone is actively looking for product specifications, give them the specifications. If someone is actively asking for a demo, show a demo. If someone is actively trying to buy from you, sell to them. The key here is that the audience *wants* to know more about buying and *wants* to buy. Sales content gets a bad rap because marketers think they can "trick" the audience into buying something.

For example, how often have you experienced a scenario like the following? You click to read a blog post from a social media site, and land on a well-written article that teaches you about the latest industry trends. At the bottom, there's a button with the call to action (CTA), "Learn more." Excited to continue learning more about the topic, you click the button, only to find that it takes you to a pricing page, a "Contact Sales" form, or a landing page with a gated asset. How frustrating!

Generic CTAs feel like a bait-and-switch, promising to help the audience learn more, but instead, forcing someone to take a buying action. This erodes trust, and results in poor lead quality, since these people were not actually ready and able to make a purchase. Instead, we should match our CTAs to the audience intent, and the intent of the next asset. For example:

- "Read article" leads the audience to a free, ungated article.
- "Watch demo" leads to a free, ungated video.
- "View pricing" leads to *actual* prices for each tier of the product or service.
- "Register for free" leads the audience to secure a seat or a ticket.
- "Contact Sales" leads to a form to share contact information with a sales representative.

Each of these CTAs tells me exactly what happens on the next screen. This leads to a better audience experience and a better sales experience because the individual knows exactly what choice they're making. It may sound counterintuitive, but giving your audience the option *not* to buy actually increases the sales close rate when someone chooses to take a buying action.

If I know that I can read an article or contact Sales, and I *choose* to contact Sales, I am much more likely to be ready, willing, and able to make a purchase. As a marketer, I'm giving my audience the option to declare explicit intent, instead of relying on assumed or implicit intent.

An unfortunate side effect of all the bait-and-switch content is that everyone thinks *everything* is a sales pitch. We often want deep examples from personal experience, but, if you mention your company, people tune out because they perceive it as selling. We want to know exactly how someone uses tools to solve problems, but, if you mention a tool your company makes, people tune out because it feels like selling. We want insights into dealing with other teams, but, if you mention your in-house colleagues and the work they do, people tune out because they see it as selling.

However, if we focus on aligning assets to audience intent, and including explicit, intent-aligned CTAs, we build trust and engage our audience. We convince them not to ignore our ideas, content, and offerings, precisely because they have the option to learn and choose whether they make a purchase or not.

Clear CTAs allow the audience to choose their path, from exploring to building trust and rapport, to learning about best practices, to starting the purchase process.

Explicit Versus Implicit Intent

Intent alignment also extends to your sales outreach and event strategy. For example, incentivized meetings have grown in popularity, as more companies try to cut through the noise. The incentivized meeting is simple: Offer something of value to potential prospects to attend a meeting with a sales representative from your company. The offers might range from sending lunch to the prospect, offering a gift card, or sending tailored gifts like shoes, wine, or books.

I would argue, though, that these tactics rely too heavily on implicit intent, and often don't result in qualified prospects attending the meeting.

As a buyer, the solution is the incentive. If I actually have the problem your company solves, I've already secured budget to purchase a solution, and I'm genuinely interested in your offering, I don't need additional reasons to book a meeting with a sales representative. I'm incentivized to solve my problem. Conversely, if I don't have the problem, or don't have time or money to buy and implement a solution, and don't have executive buy-in for either the problem or the solution, a lunch or a pair of shoes is not going to change those facts. For senior-level decision-makers, the value of the gift is often much too small to reflect the value you're asking them to give the sales representative.

These meetings are often billed as a "15-minute call" or "quick lunch meeting," but we know that the salesperson sends an email to follow up. And they might start reaching out to other members of the prospect's team, with phrasing like, "I met with Ashley the other day…" or "I was just talking to Ashley, and she mentioned…" in order to build trust. But, the incentives and follow-up are misaligned if the recipient does not have the intent to make a purchase. If you want to use an incentive to build the relationship, focus on the "build" and "maintain" phases, not the "start" phase. Consider these three scenarios:

- **I was looking to purchase a SaaS tool, and was deliberating between two industry leaders.** My sales representative invited me to a dinner with other prospects and current customers. There were six attendees at the table, with two high-level leaders of the company and the representative trying to sell to us. I was able to ask detailed questions of the leader and other users and prospects about which tools they considered, what challenges they needed to solve, and why they leaned towards this company's offering. Yes, it was a nice meal, but the real value was access to all those people in one place in comparison to a reference call, and making new professional connections with people trying to solve similar problems. I bought that software.

- **Send a welcome gift after a deal closes.** Basically, it's a token that says, "We look forward to doing business together, and we're committed to your success." When I worked in-person in an office, many of our staffing agencies and creative agencies sent treat baskets, which I then shared with all my teammates and told them all about the deal and the vendor. That meant I wasn't the only person who knew them and liked them—in case I would no longer be the person who made the decision.

- **I've worked with a vendor who provides video editing services for several years.** An account manager has been working with one-off teams because I introduce them when my colleagues need the services they provide. This account manager proactively started the conversation about consolidating the contract to become our vendor of choice by telling me how much we could have saved if we had bought in bulk up-front rather than the one-off purchases every few months. They win because now they're the top vendor for their services in our system, and we win because we get a discount for buying more. In this case, the "incentive" wasn't lunch or gifts, it was starting the conversation earlier and connecting the dots that I didn't necessarily see because I didn't manage the relationship or budget for every team.

In each case, the incentive matched the explicit intent, and the sales representatives were able to move the conversation forward, build the relationship, and ultimately, grow the business.

I've used this tactic at in-person events as well. A common tactic to increase booth traffic is to offer the best giveaway on the show floor. Booths might run raffles for high-ticket items or request a badge scan in exchange for the coveted giveaway, but how likely are these "leads" to convert to post-event follow-ups? Instead, I take a slightly provocative approach: I explicitly ask people why they stopped at the booth. My questions are: Are you here to learn about [our offering], just here for the giveaway, or did you happen to stop here but are actually looking for directions to somewhere else?

This approach saves us both time! If they only want the giveaway and we don't have an explicit barrier to taking it, I just give them the item and let them go on their way. I don't need to add junk to my post-event follow-up campaigns if someone has zero interest in our offering. For the folks who are interested in our offering, it's worth giving them the attention to explain features and benefits, show them a demo, and answer their questions. This might mean that I can't give attention to other people who enter the booth, so I need to make sure it's worth my time to focus on this person. Giving attendees the option to take the giveaway and leave or stay for a deep conversation about our offering is beneficial for both of us! And for the folks who just happened to stop in front of our booth en route to another location, it doesn't hurt to be helpful. Who knows? Maybe they turn out to be interested in the offering, looking for a partnership opportunity, or job hunting, and there's an exchange of value that makes sense for both sides.

Search Intent: Keyword-Driven vs. Keyword-Aligned vs. Keyword-Informed

Marketers often talk about "search intent" as part of their content strategy, using search engine optimization (SEO) as a basis for their content. Our goal is to create content to educate our audience, so we need to make sure they can find that content. SEO helps with findability and helps ensure that the audience search intent matches the content they receive.

While SEO is a key part of executing certain assets, it's not the core driver of a content strategy. Thus, we need to discuss the intersection of SEO and intent-based content, using three SEO approaches: keyword-driven, keyword-aligned, and keyword-informed.

Keyword-driven strategy focuses on capturing the highest placement on the search engine results page (SERP) for as many high monthly search volume (MSV) keywords as possible. This approach results in a long list of high-MSV keywords, simply to generate a ton of traffic to company pages. Unfortunately, this tactic might attract the wrong audience. Because the highest-volume keywords are often basic queries, like "what is [topic]?" or "define [concept]," the audience who searches these queries likely does not have a buying intent. Similarly, generic "head" terms have high MSV, but unclear search intent, and likely no buying intent. While more traffic is good, it's not useful if it won't convert, since the audience intent is unclear, or, at best, only learn-intent. Unfortunately, the audience is likely agnostic about who answers their query, and the "featured snippet" or preview summaries on the SERP often mean that the searcher does not click to a company site.

Keyword-driven content is rarely beneficial for mature companies, and simply focusing on high-MSV keywords is a losing strategy, particularly as more AI-created content floods the internet. However, we *do* need to make sure we use language and answer questions in a way that our target audience understands. Thus, we want to be keyword-aligned and keyword-informed to ensure the right audience finds the right content.

Keyword-aligned content takes into account the audience needs and the business needs, including converting buy-intent searches into pipeline or revenue. In order to move the conversation forward, we need to be in the existing conversation. Keyword alignment helps us find those conversations, and helps people searching for information around those conversations find us.

Even in nascent markets, the problem the company has identified exists (otherwise, we wouldn't bother building an offering to take to market), so we need to ensure that we make our new ideas and offerings findable. Keyword-aligned content looks at more niche keywords within the topic to understand how the audience talks about the problem and solution spaces, and how they search for information about these topics. Instead of chasing the highest-MSV keywords, the marketer chooses the most relevant keywords, and matches the topics that the audience cares about with the topics the company cares about.

Keyword-informed content is an extension of keyword-aligned content, and helps the marketer expand their library of keywords and topics related to their initial list. Tools like Ahrefs, Semrush, and BrightEdge recommend adjacent keywords to help marketers see a broader picture of the topic they wish to address. Google's "people also ask" feature in the SERP is a helpful way to gain keyword-informed insights to shape future content. For example, imagine that you're trying to sell a software product to platform engineers to help them manage dependencies in a sprawling, distributed cloud environment. In a keyword-driven approach, you might chase the term "microservices", because it boasts a high MSV. However, the intent is too broad, and covers a wide variety of entry-level concepts, such as "define microservices" and "what a microservice is," while the audience who actually needs the product is quite experienced, and already knows this information.

A keyword-aligned approach matches the language of the problem for the audience, with clear titles, headers (H1, H2, and so on), and descriptions. For example, an article about how to decompose a monolith into microservices might include the following H2: "Step 1: Map your existing architecture." This helps the humans and the search algorithms parse the content, ensuring that it's more relevant to a sophisticated searcher's intent.

As we noted, we want to match searcher and business needs. This means that, in many cases, we want the content to attract buy- or use-intent audiences. Continuing the platform engineering example, this means that we prioritize content with a title like "Tools to improve platform engineering workflows" or "Rituals to accelerate shipping software" over a general "How I became a platform engineer" article. In the first two titles, we see clear buy-intent and use-intent angles for the content, compared to the third title, which does not easily map to a strong business outcome for a company selling a software tool.

Time Horizon

We need a combination of evergreen and timely content for the audience.

Some channels require a more consistent publishing cadence, while others remain more static. Most social media platforms reward publishing consistently, but this does differ among the platforms and formats. For example, in 2024, LinkedIn generally rewarded less-frequent publishing than X (Twitter), while Instagram rewarded reels more than text posts. However, algorithms change on each platform, and new entrants, like TikTok and Threads, change the way users consume and engage with different types of content across each platform. Thus, we need to be mindful of which assets we include in our journey. For journeys meant to build trust, we likely want to include more evergreen content, with links to living channels for people to explore timely content. In contrast, an onboarding journey for a product with frequent updates requires timely content as the product changes. Service providers, like creative agencies and strategic consultants, need to stay on top of craft best practices, industry trends, and market shifts in order to offer relevant advice and deliverables to their clients.

Practically, this affects how we use time stamps and publishing dates, phrasing about "series" or "recent," and when we need to refresh content to ensure that it meets audience needs. Refreshing content might include updating statistics and source citations, refreshing product screenshots, and adding links to other resources.

This also affects how we map our narratives for conferences, press pitches or briefings, and other events, including podcasts or webinars. Outlets with a more formal pitching or publishing process often want net-new content. For example, a large industry conference might be the perfect place to unveil new research or survey data, so timing the publishing dates and additional assets to coincide with the industry conference might be a key part of your distribution strategy.

As you consider creating, refreshing, and sunsetting key narratives, factor in the long-tail distribution potential of making a change. Many teams use the calendar year or the fiscal year to drive planning, but the key moments for your audience should also inform publishing and distribution roadmaps.

Mapping Assets and Channels

You'll notice that the frameworks here make little mention of specific asset types and channels, and no mention of organic or paid distribution tactics. Most assets and channels do not have an inherent intent. As marketers, we designate the intent for each asset. We may choose to focus certain channels on certain intents, but these are generally not universal (with the exception of spaces where the intent is implicit in the definition, such as "Product tour," "Buyer's Guide," "Help Center," or "Supporting documentation").

For example, a blog post does *not* inherently mean learn-intent content. A video does *not* inherently mean use-intent content. Social media does *not* inherently mean conceptual content. A forum post does *not* inherently mean tactical content. We need to define our intents and depths as we create content for the entire journey. We can have multiple assets addressing the same depth or intent, and we can use many different formats to address each depth and intent.

Further, *each asset does not need to address all depths in a single deliverable*. Often, addressing conceptual, strategic, and tactical depths in a single asset makes it too dense and difficult to consume for most audience members. Such an asset is often referred to as "pillar content," "hub content," or an "ultimate guide." The marketer then breaks this asset into multiple assets to create a journey, addressing different depths via multiple channels and formats.

This goes beyond simply regurgitating the asset in different formats. For example, a basic tactic is to take the transcript from a podcast and publish it as a blog post. Another basic tactic is to publish the slide deck from a conference presentation as a LinkedIn carousel. In both cases, the creator makes few or no edits, and the asset depth and intent stay the same.

Instead, we want to think about *modular content*. How can we share the information in multiple ways by strategically separating or combining the content in an asset, tailored to the new format and the distribution channel? (We'll discuss detailed tactics to create modular content in Chapter 4.)

As we think about depths versus funnel stages, we realize that we need to *allow people to immediately dive deeper, or pop back up if they need more context*. A single team does not need to own every asset and channel, and we don't need to use every asset available in "official" or "formal" journeys. Two examples that might not have a specific asset included in the journey map are a community forum (such as Reddit, Quora, or a company-run online community) and LinkedIn.

Community forum content includes information from multiple sources, with variety in credibility, depth, and accuracy. This content also tends to focus on more timely topics rather than evergreen information. Thus, community posts are less likely to be included in a formal journey, managed by a lifecycle or demand-generation marketing team.

Similarly, social media platforms like LinkedIn focus more on conversations among people on the platform. The content is quite ephemeral, and most platforms don't lend themselves to robust searching or content organization. It's intended to be conversational and timely, so we prefer to link to the overall account rather than trying to include a specific post in a formal journey.

If we see that a series on a community forum gained a lot of traction, it would probably be beneficial to aggregate the series into a more evergreen asset for a better audience experience. If we see that a certain topic gained significant interest on social media, it would probably be beneficial to consider a more robust asset on the topic (like a blog post or YouTube video).

As you can see, "content" is a broad term, encompassing many asset types, including written (long-form or short-form), visual, audio, or interactive. Outlets include paid, owned, and earned platforms, as well as a place to host and share content. The traditional funnel emphasizes owned platforms, as hosting gated content helps to track leads and conversions. Your audience, however, spends time on a variety of non-owned platforms, and their next action might not be a buying action, so consider which metrics you want to optimize for each asset on each platform.

A HOLISTIC APPROACH TO DISTRIBUTION

The following are some tactics to take a holistic approach to your distribution strategy:

- Choose platforms based on industry research from analysts like Gartner and Forrester, benchmarking data from academia and consulting firms like MIT, Harvard Business Review, Deloitte, and McKinsey, and surveys of your audience. You can also test different platforms to understand how your audience interacts with that platform.

- Look at communities where your audience spends time. For example, developers spend time and engage on Reddit and HackerNews. Lifestyle brands are often showcased on Instagram.

- Ask your target audience where they spend time when you meet them at events, and include open-ended questions about content consumption in your customer surveys.

- Conduct broad searches on Google, YouTube, and relevant social media channels to understand what information your audience might be searching for, who holds the top search results, and how much engagement each outlet generates. The key is to think beyond the standard SEO keywords that you already target, and instead try to tap into the emerging conversations happening among your audiences.

Fitness: An Example to Demonstrate the Concepts

Let's look at an example of how we apply content depths and intents to our content. I love using fitness as a general way of explaining these concepts, because most people have some understanding of the foundational elements of fitness.

Let's break it down: What does it mean to be healthy and fit? Most people agree that it's some combination of diet and exercise. But, if we apply the content depths, depending on the brand and product objectives, we see that the answers to that question vary, based on the audience. Think about how the answers change if you're *Muscle & Fitness* magazine or *Runner's World*, or *Yoga Journal*.

Let's say we're answering the question as *Muscle & Fitness* magazine. From a *journey perspective*, let's say an audience member scrolls Pinterest, and sees a recipe for chicken stir fry (tactical, use-intent). They click the link and land on the recipe section of the *Muscle & Fitness* website. The opening line of the blog about the chicken stir fry recipe states, "Protein is essential to building more muscle." This sentence links "protein is essential" to a conceptual-level article discussing the benefits of a high-protein diet (conceptual, learn-intent). The conceptual article includes an embedded video about fast- versus slow-digesting protein (strategic, learn-intent content). At the bottom of the article is a CTA with three different types of protein supplement (tactical, buy-intent content).

As the user jumps down to the ingredients, several are hyperlinked to buy via an affiliate link (tactical, buy-intent). The related content at the bottom links to five more chicken dinner recipes (tactical, use-intent). There's a sidebar CTA to read an article about balancing your macros (strategic, learn-intent content) and another sidebar CTA to buy a monthly meal-planning template from the site (tactical, buy-intent content). Let's say the user purchases the meal-planning template. It then includes links to a blog post with a roundup of recipes related to each ingredient (tactical, use-intent).

We see here that *funnel phases are not the same as content depths*, and that the *intent for each asset is different*. If you already know that protein is essential for building muscle, you don't click the link to the conceptual content, but your journey remains clear and helpful. You can use the meal-planning template without exploring the recipes or buying the ingredients from the affiliate links. You can buy protein supplements without buying the meal-planning template.

It's also possible to change the depth of an asset, based on the angle you use when discussing it. For example, the meal-planning template in this example is tactical, buy-intent content. But we could up-level "meal planning" to strategic content by talking about how it's useful to create the right habits, different tactics for meal-planning (including the meal-planning template), and how to use meal-planning to achieve your overall health goals. Alternatively, "meal planning" could become multiple tactical assets if we narrow the focus. For example, "meal planning for peak week before a competition," "meal planning for reverse dieting," "meal planning for muscle growth," "meal planning for fat loss," and "meal planning for maintenance." In all cases, we could include the buy-intent CTA for a tactical meal-planning template.

We also see the *time horizons for different content depths*. The concept of big, strong muscles and a high-protein diet as markers of health remain relevant for many years. Meanwhile, the strategic ideas of good form while lifting and consuming different sources of protein might change as we learn more about how the human body works, or as science progresses to produce more protein-heavy options. Similarly, the tactics can change weekly, with new recipes or exercises frequently available.

Explicit CTAs are essential to making this journey seamless. If every CTA said, "Learn more," that's not helpful. Does the audience learn more about each supplement, or will they go to a place where they can add these supplements to a cart to make a purchase? Instead, we acknowledge that *we're not tricking anyone into buying* anything. "See all supplements" or "Buy now" directly under a single supplement are much clearer CTAs. "Explore recipes" or "Buy ingredients" help the audience understand what happens next when they tap a button or a link.

If we apply this mindset to the assets created by most business-to-business (B2B) companies, we see discrepancies. "Read the ebook" results in a landing page with a form. "Learn more" takes you to the homepage of a product tour. "Get access" can lead to a login page, a generic community group that doesn't require logging in, or a product sign-up flow.

REAL-WORLD EXAMPLE   Atlassian Team Playbook

Atlassian is a collaboration software maker, on a mission to unleash the potential of every team. The company focuses on maximizing team health, improving ways of working, and increasing productivity among teams of all types.

It commissions surveys, conducts original research, and runs experiments to fuel trust-intent content. These insights fuel conceptual-depth, trust- or learn-intent assets. These assets form the foundation of the thought leadership content, on a site where they share a unique and opinionated perspective on teamwork. The findings from the research and experiments are used to craft "plays" for the Atlassian Team Playbook, which includes exercises and worksheets to help teams work better together.[1]

The site includes a mix of strategic- and tactical-depth content, with a combination of learn-intent and use-intent assets. For example, the Team Health Monitor is a strategic, use-intent asset. It focuses on five to seven key factors of a healthy team. The team comes together with a facilitator to run the Team Health Monitor play, giving a thumbs up, thumbs sideways, or thumbs down to indicate agreement or disagreement on each indicator of team health. For example, one indicator is, "Every project has an owner, and we know who the owner is." If a teammate agrees with this statement, they give a thumbs up. Once they score each indicator, the team uses the Health Monitor prompt questions to dive into areas of strength and areas for improvement.

The Health Monitor also calls out pitfalls. The "project owner" question, for instance, includes a follow-up that every teammate should name the project owner. If it turns out that people gave a thumbs up to knowing the owner, but each teammate names a different owner, the facilitator realizes that, in fact, they need to dig into this area to identify and document project ownership. This might lead them to use the DACI play (Driver, Approver, Contributor, and Informed). This asset is tactical, use-intent content.

While these assets are meant to help the audience improve their ways of working, many of the plays have product tie-ins. The DACI play includes a template in the company's knowledge management product, Confluence. The Retrospective play includes a template in one of its project management tools, Trello. You don't need to purchase the products to receive value from the content, and you don't need to give your email that ends up in a buy-intent nurture campaign in order to access the content, but this is an excellent example of allowing the audience to chart their own journey. They can learn at multiple depths, use the plays for tactical improvements, and explore the products if they're interested.

Conclusion: The Playground Mindset Shift

Taking a strategic approach to building the playground requires a lot of work! This is the part that makes marketing challenging and fun. We take on the cognitive load of creating many touchpoints, mapping them all out, and matching substance, assets, and channels to audience needs.

Our audience shouldn't feel the pain of wading through all of the different decisions to determine depth, intent, time horizon, asset types, and channels. Instead, our job as marketers is to make it feel effortless for the audience to find, consume, and act on the content we provide. This means that we don't try to force a learn-intent search query down a buy-intent path, and we don't make someone sit through the conceptual what and why of an idea if they're interested in purchasing a tactical solution.

The playground mindset meets the audience where they are. If they've done their research and they're ready to buy, we sell, immediately. If they're just starting to think about the edges of a problem space, we educate. If they're a loyal user looking for more ways to solve problems with our product, we offer tactical, use-intent content to make it easy.

The best marketers know that it's not just about attracting short-term attention. Attention is fleeting, and marketers need to focus on holding the audience's attention in order to guide a journey that educates, empowers, and converts, no matter which path someone takes.

Chapter Summary

- We are building a playground, which means we need to shift our mindset as we map out our content strategy.

- Map content to three depths: conceptual (the what and why of the idea), strategic (key processes, tools, and knowledge components), and tactical (the how, including step-by-step instructions and templates or exercises).

- Focus on intent-based content, thinking about the next action the audience will take after consuming the content. Key intents include trust, buy, use, help, and learn.

- Explicit intent is more indicative of audience intention, so use explicit CTAs and avoid the generic "learn more."

- Consider the time horizon for different asset types and channels as you make decisions about names, time stamps, and publishing cadence.

Note

1 Atlassian (2024) *Atlassian Team Playbook*, atlassian.cc/team-playbook (archived at https://perma.cc/5W8J-4TLS)

Tactics to Increase Reach, Engagement, and Conversion

04

To maximize the reach, engagement, and impact of content, marketers need to create modular content. Modular content allows teams to create multiple assets from a single asset, combine assets in different formats, and match assets to each distribution channel. Content must be shaped with long-tail, multi-channel distribution in mind.

As we saw with the fitness example in Chapter 3, your audience consumes content in many ways, across many different channels. How do you ensure your content is available where they consume and engage, with seamless handoffs throughout the journey?

To accomplish this, we need lots of assets in many different channels. Unfortunately, no matter how big the team or how large the budget, most marketing teams don't have enough resources to do it all. This means we need to think smarter about the strategy of the journey and about deploying our resources for content creation and distribution.

Repurposing Content: From Snackable to Modular

You've probably heard that "attention spans are shorter than ever" and "audiences won't pay attention to long content." These beliefs gave rise to "snackable" content: short, bite-sized content assets, meant to be consumed in quick bursts. But snackable content assumes that content-repurposing efforts focus solely on breaking long-form content into short-form content, and this often results in *watered-down* assets, with the primary goal of driving clicks to an owned property. Unfortunately, this significantly limits the reach and resonance of your content.

Instead, marketers need to create modular content. Modular content means that you can mix and match asset types, content depths, intents, and channels.

Decomposition Versus Building Blocks

Modular content is not just about breaking long content into short content. There are two ways to approach content creation: decomposition and building blocks.

Decomposition happens when you start with one big piece of content, and then "decompose" it by splitting it into multiple assets for each distribution channel.

Benefits of the decomposition approach include:

- Cohesive narrative, since all content flows from the same initial piece of content
- Easy editorial calendar, since you're simply matching assets with channels for most of the quarter, half, or annual planning cycle.

Pitfalls of the decomposition approach include:

- The initial piece of content is *a lot* of work up front. Many subject-matter experts don't make time to invest in such a big effort all at once, many teams don't have the budget to invest in a large asset, and, if you're starting from scratch, you must wait to see results.
- If you make the wrong bet about market relevance, it's a struggle to pivot, due to the heavy investment of time and money.

The building blocks approach allows you to start with small pieces of content and bring them all together once you generate enough content to make a bigger asset.

Benefits of the building blocks approach include:

- It's more scalable up front, since you can ask multiple subject-matter experts to contribute in small batches.
- It's faster and easier to experiment to see what works in the market, which channels perform better, and which asset types resonate with your audience.

Pitfalls of the building blocks approach include:

- It's more difficult to maintain a cohesive narrative, since assets are created in smaller, faster batches.
- Individual assets might not fit into a big piece later, since the assets were created with different distribution methods, voice, and tone.

Most teams use a mix of decomposition and building blocks. Throughout the rest of the chapter, we'll discuss tactics that can be used for each method.

Content Pairing

Content pairing can be used in several ways, across content depths, asset types, and distribution channels.

Consider pairing content at two different depths. For example, Duarte, a communications agency that specializes in presentations and training, used this tactic to talk about using humor in presentations. Nancy Duarte shared an article on LinkedIn talking about how humor helps presenters resonate with their audience (strategic depth). She noted different ways to include humor in presentations, and then paired the article with a carousel of examples of well-known speakers and comedians using each type of humor (tactical depth).[1]

She also paired two pieces of strategic-depth content in different assets when she was promoting her book, Illuminate (co-authored with Patti Sanchez).[2] The book speaks about the stories that leaders need to tell on a transformation journey (conceptual depth), with 10 key stories noted in the book (strategic depth). Nancy and Patti created two carousels, one with five Motivating Stories, and the other with five Warning Stories. These carousels were distributed on Slideshare and

LinkedIn, and repurposed into long-form blog posts on the company website. Each asset included a CTA to buy the book or explore the Duarte course-offering related to the book. Nancy also gave high-level overviews of these story types when presenting at in-person conferences, and sent links to the blogs or carousels in the follow-up emails to session attendees.

If you have a robust hub for housing assets, you can pair multiple assets types and content depths. For example, collaboration-software maker Atlassian shares content across the conceptual, strategic, and tactical depth on its Agile microsite. The site includes long-form written content and short videos about topics related to the Agile manifesto, principles, and methodology. The articles are optimized for high-search-volume keywords to drive organic traffic from search engines, and the video titles are optimized to capture traffic and attention via YouTube. Videos are embedded into relevant articles, and articles are linked from the descriptions of the YouTube videos. This allows the audience to find the content via search or YouTube, consume it in their preferred format, and explore it at the most relevant depth.

In both of these examples, the asset includes a buy-intent CTA in portions of the learn-intent content. For example, after reading any of the assets about storytelling from Duarte, the reader can immediately implement the suggestions, without making a purchase. If they want to dive deeper, or need help implementing the solution, they can purchase the book or a course. The Atlassian team showcased relevant product features by mapping them back to Agile principles. For example, building a backlog is an essential task for agile teams. Jira offers a feature that allows teams to build a backlog, so a tutorial "Build a backlog in Jira" is included as the CTA in the article "What is a backlog?" The article was a learn-intent, tactical-depth piece, which linked to a use-intent, tactical piece.

Content Syndication

Paid syndication is a tried-and-true tactic in the marketing mix, but many teams forget about second- and third-run content (and beyond). They also think about keeping the content intact, but syndication can work in tandem with content pairing. For example, pairing a problem and solution, and syndicating each piece across multiple paid or organic channels. The Muse, a career site, used this tactic to reach new audiences on LinkedIn. One of its editors wrote a LinkedIn article about standing out as a candidate. She shared the story of rejecting a candidate based on their résumé. It turns out that this candidate was a referral from a current employee, who asked the hiring manager to reconsider. They ended up interviewing, and ultimately hiring, the candidate they originally rejected. The LinkedIn article linked to a piece on The Muse site with tips to make sure that this wouldn't happen to future candidates.

This tactic also works with research. You can talk about the problem, what it is, and why it matters in one piece of content, and create a separate asset to share details about the results of the research. You can also republish entire articles as sponsored content for paid syndication, or as second- or third-run content on organic sites. For example, Atlassian republishes some of its technical articles on DZone, a publication with a developer audience. The site allows companies to republish educational content and includes a backlink to the original piece of content. This allows authors to extend their reach to new audiences and generate links to owned content.

Similarly, syndication is not just for written content. Sites like Vimeo and YouTube allow you to curate playlists, with algorithms and search results, just like SEO tactics for written content.

COPE: Create Once, Publish Everywhere

I love the acronym COPE, which stands for Create once, publish everywhere. I learned this saying from a colleague who works with digital asset management and content management systems, which help teams organize assets to make it easier to distribute and update content across multiple external platforms.

Marketers take this idea a few steps further by editing the content to help extend the reach and impact. In order to create modular content effectively, marketers need to think holistically about potential asset types and long-tail distribution.

The following list provides a few suggestions, along with examples, to help you expand conference content:

- Sections of a conference deck—LinkedIn carousels

- Speaker notes from a conference deck—LinkedIn copy and slide image
- Animation from a conference deck—Instagram reel, YouTube short, X (Twitter) video
- X thread with commentary—Long-form article
- Long-form article—Parse sections into several tweet threads or text-only LinkedIn posts
- Video—Transcript becomes a long-form article
- Podcast—Community post of key takeaways.

For example, I turn my presentation slides into LinkedIn carousels. I update the post copy with a slightly different angle each time, which keeps the content fresh, while allowing me to extend the reach of a core idea and asset. The content depths are also referenced in my Four Pillars of Thought Leadership framework (introduced in Chapter 9).

If we continue the fitness example from Chapter 3, we see that we can remix assets into different formats. It's not just turning a long-form written blog about recipes into a short carousel of a subset of the recipes. If, for example, you're *Muscle & Fitness* magazine, you might share a series of instructional videos or short articles with exercises for specific muscle groups. Those assets can then be compiled into an ultimate guide or paired to create a weekly workout plan.

Another easy tactic to extend the shelf life of an asset is to take the opposite view of the original piece. For example, if you have an article titled, "Five tips to improve project delivery times," you can share "Five mistakes that impact project delivery times." If the tips include suggestions to break the project down into smaller tasks, set milestones for each task, and have regular check-ins to ensure everyone is on track, the opposite article might include not breaking the project down into smaller tasks, setting a single deadline, and spacing out check-ins. You can generate an additional piece of content from this core idea by creating an asset that combines the two perspectives and offers solutions. The title might be "Project delivery times: Pitfalls to avoid, and tips to accelerate your timelines."

Not all content is suitable for distribution in the same asset type. For example, live panels from an event generally don't film well, and it's difficult to trim them into clips. Instead, using the recording to generate a transcript to edit into a written asset is a better treatment for panel content.

Customer presentations tend to suffer the same fate as panels. Many customers struggle to offer unique reasons for why they purchased the product or service, and they tend to share high-level, often similar, use cases. Thus, instead of sharing multiple 45-minute customer presentations that might be redundant, this content might be better reimagined into a carousel or one-page PDF of reasons why customers choose you. This works particularly well for industries with focused verticals. For example, if you share three customer presentations in the finance and banking industry, you might create an asset titled, "Why Wells Fargo, Northwestern Mutual, and Chase Bank chose [Company]," or "How Morgan Stanley, Bank of America, and Credit Suisse [saved money or saved time] with [Product]," or "Increasing security and compliance in regulated industries: Real-world examples from Mastercard, Visa, and CitiGroup." This allows you to amplify customer voices, offer social proof, and show specialization in an industry, without repeating the same value props over and over again in a duplicative set of assets.

Live demos or use-case walk-throughs generally don't make great written assets, since they're so focused on showcasing the product. Screenshots are blurred or too small in a downloadable PDF, and it's often much more difficult to present the content via still screenshots in a PDF as opposed to animations. While a web page or blog post solves the animation issue, it results in an exceptionally long scroll depth and, potentially, slow page-load speeds. In sum, as a key repurposing tactic, live demos are best translated into a video format or other image-focused format, not into written assets.

Round-ups or summaries also work well for social media threads and discussions in comments or forums. Funky Marketing, an agency that works with B2B companies, uses this tactic across LinkedIn and blog posts. Nemanja Zivkovic, the founder, has a large, engaged following on LinkedIn. He asks questions about industry challenges and trends and turns the replies into a long-form blog, formatting quotes from the thread as images throughout the blog. He adds his unique point of view, and then shares the long-form blog back to his LinkedIn feed, tagging all the contributors that he featured from the original comment thread. This is smart because he's validating the ideas with actual comments from real people in his feed and increasing engagement by tagging the people he featured.

Shaping Content for Modular Content and Long-Tail Distribution

In order to create modular content, you need to shape the content with long-tail distribution and multiple asset types and content depths in mind. The following sections detail practical ways to make it easier to use decomposition and building-block techniques to extend the usability, reach, and impact of your content.

Images

Think of a couple of key messages that you would love to see shared around on LinkedIn or included as a hero image on a round-up blog. These should become slides in some way. The message could be words, a chart, a big statistic, a diagram, or whatever, but it needs to be a static image that stays on the screen long enough to be a screenshot or a picture. And it needs to include enough context that it can stand on its own or pair with minimal copy.

Animations are great for live presentations, but if you don't leave enough time for the complete animation, or it happens over several minutes of speaking, it's hard to pull out a static image. Slides that are extremely wordy result in a bad audience experience *and* are generally poor for image posts on social media, unusable for hero images with the press, and so on.

Tactical Tips to Make it Easier to Create Images

Think about your conference stage shots. These can make great social media posts and/or images for blog posts or articles about the conference. For example, when I present about treating the audience journey as a playground, I include a slide that reads, "Treat the buyer's journey as a playground: People can enter and exit as they please, they can go in any order, and they can engage with content the 'wrong' way." The slide contains enough context to understand that I've introduced a new concept, and it gets you thinking, even if you're not 100 per cent sure what I mean by "playground." This can be paired with LinkedIn copy, used as an opening quote in a blog post, or shared by attendees with their own takeaways from the session.

Video

For many teams, video continues to be a highly requested asset type and content format across multiple channels, but most audience members and platforms prefer shorter clips. Thus, marketers usually try to edit down longer sessions for quick consumption.

Remember: You don't need to tell the whole story with every asset! You can tee up a concept and then link to the longer recording or a long-form written article. You can show the steps to solve a problem, and link to a high-level discussion of the problem space or solution space.

Tactical Tips for Video Content

Here are a few guidelines on length, depending on the platform:

- **Social media:** Some platforms enforce hard time limits of either 30 seconds or 60 seconds. If the platform does not enforce a length restriction, shorter is still better. For a snippet from a longer session, aim to keep these clips under two minutes.

- **Ads:** Lengths vary from 15 to 60 seconds. People rarely say something very useful in that amount of time, unless they are specifically scripted to do so. If you want to turn content from a live event into an ad, you need to make sure the speaker has a succinct script that they can say cleanly.

- **Article embed:** This is a great way to pair content and give the audience a choice of consumption options and content depths. This is a commonly used tactic, and the videos can be 2 to 10 minutes long.

- **Community or forum post:** You can embed the full video or include snippets, paired with a written summary of key takeaways. This is also a great way to generate discussion and engagement among your audience.

It's particularly important to consider the long-tail distribution of video assets, since they're more difficult to edit at a later date. A growing use case for AI tools is clipping shorter snippets from longer videos, but most people don't naturally say smart things within 30- or 60-second time limits! This makes it difficult to create shorter clips, for both AI and human editors. Thus, if you know you want short snippets from a longer video, you need to build soundbites into the script, and key slides or imagery in the visuals.

Common pitfalls include:

- Opening with, "In this series…" or "In Part 1, we'll cover…" This makes it difficult to let the video stand alone or to embed it in articles. It also obligates you to create additional related content, and makes it more difficult to update content if it's referenced specifically in other videos.

- Referring to pronouns instead of naming the nouns. In live presentations, speakers often state the company or product name at the beginning of the presentation, but refer to "we" or "it" in later slides. This makes it difficult to cut a short snippet, because the viewer lacks context of who "we" are or what "it" is. You can remedy this by including the company or offering name on the slide, having succinct section intros or summaries, or building nouns into the original script.

- Using time-sensitive or location-dependent greetings or references. This is common in live presentations, where the speaker opens with, "Welcome to [Conference], I'm excited to be here this morning!" or "Good morning, it's a beautiful day here in [City]!" If speakers keep these to openings or closings, it's much easier to make clips from the video, but speakers should keep these references to a minimum if they intend to use the content for post-event campaigns.

- Referencing other speakers or previous slides, without giving context. For example, instead of saying, "As I mentioned earlier…"

or "As we saw a few slides ago..." say, "If we agree that [core concept from earlier in the talk] is true, then [new information you're about to share]." Again, if the viewer doesn't have access to the entire talk, they lack context for references to "earlier" or "a few slides ago."

Written Content

Some companies do a good job with this content type, but I've seen examples from longer recordings where the speaker is a bit all over the place. In this case, I would argue that the written asset reflects poor presentation structure, and marketers should partner with the speaker to fix the presentation, because the live audience is probably confused as well.

In addition, there are more options than a downloadable PDF or a long-form blog post. Don't forget about backlinks and cross-linking, parsing content out into a one-pager, and/or mid-form content, such as on LinkedIn and community or forum posts.

Tactical Tips for Written Content

- **Batch your examples or metaphors**: Either use the same example throughout or match your examples to a single concept, and avoid reusing the same example in different areas of the presentation. For example, when I talk about content depths, I use the fitness example to demonstrate all three depths. Later in the presentation, I use examples from companies to showcase a single depth or single channel. I don't bring up fitness again in those examples to avoid confusing my audience. If you're going to use a metaphor, use the same metaphor for the entire presentation. Don't start with a race car, then move to a boat, then to a fruit bowl, then back to a boat.

- **Edit from a transcript**: Get a head start on writing assets with a recording and transcript from a rehearsal. You don't actually need the final presentation recording to start drafting, assuming the speaker has a solid story to rehearse ahead of time. Use tools like Loom, Otter.ai, and Rev for cheap and fast machine-generated transcripts to kick-start the writing process afterwards.

- **Content depths:** I mentioned content depths earlier in the chapter, but this topic comes up frequently with event content. We don't need multiple conceptual- or strategic-depth written assets. We can generally pair multiple tactical-depth assets to a few conceptual or strategic assets. The speaker might need to give an overview of the problem space and/or solution space in a live talk, but, if we have already covered that in an existing asset, we can focus on the new tactical pieces and link to existing assets that cover conceptual or strategic content.

Infographics

Infographics are another highly requested asset type, but they aren't often created, largely because many teams don't generally create content that lends itself to becoming an infographic. Infographics work best when you have information that benefits from data visualization. Simply putting a set of numbers in a long vertical orientation with some illustrations is *not* an infographic, and it rarely makes the information easier to understand or consume. If you want to create an infographic, you need data that benefits from visualization.

For some excellent examples of data visualization and infographics, try the Gapminder website. Gapminder is an independent Swedish foundation whose mission is to fight devastating misconceptions with a fact-based worldview everyone can understand. Gapminder uses a variety of data visualization tools to break down complex topics and weave interconnected variables into cohesive insights. Because it aims to promote a fact-based worldview, it's critical that the audience sees the information presented as accurate and unbiased, and can easily understand the collection methods and relationships between each piece of data. For example, an interactive data visualization on the homepage uses a range of circles of multiple sizes, colors, and axis labels to help the audience understand differences in income, life expectancy, and gross domestic product (GDP) in different regions. Simply showing this information in a series of individual bar charts or tables, or writing out long paragraphs with numbers, would make it much more difficult to parse the information. Gapminder has done the hard work of translating the data into a comprehensive visual so that its audience can more easily understand the information.

Due to the abstraction required, data visualization and infographics have high potential for mistakes, which means your audience is likely to be more skeptical of information showcased in this style. In order to maintain trust, think carefully about how best to showcase factual, unbiased data.

REAL-WORLD EXAMPLE   HubSpot INBOUND

HubSpot began as a marketing automation platform (MAP), and, over the years, expanded to include a customer relationship management (CRM) system, as well as tools for operations, content marketing, customer service, and more.

Its flagship conference, INBOUND, has grown to become one of the largest marketing conferences in the United States, and attracts thousands of attendees each year. HubSpot still uses INBOUND as the platform for major product and feature releases, company announcements (such as strategic partnerships or leadership updates), and gathering fans, customers, press, and analysts in its target cohorts.

But INBOUND has grown beyond HubSpot. What started as a user conference grew into its own brand, platforms, and audience. For this reason, the HubSpot team chose to create an entire strategy around the INBOUND brand, the content created for and related to the conference, and the expert speakers who speak at the conference. For example, it created LinkedIn, X, Facebook, TikTok, and Instagram pages for INBOUND, sharing photos from the event, teasers about the upcoming speaker line-up, and content from past speakers.

Alongside this, the INBOUND blog features recaps from popular sessions. It also gives speakers an additional platform to share more about their topics by bylining blogs, which are then shared to the INBOUND social platforms and its newsletter. *The Insider by INBOUND* newsletter features speaker-bylined content on different themes, such as customer marketing and content marketing. It's also a marketing tool to attract repeat attendees to the event, with early-bird ticket pricing and sneak-peek announcements in the CTAs.

The authors also have the ability to share this content in their personal channels, generating additional reach not only for their topic, but also for the INBOUND brand. These channels create a symbiotic relationship with the speakers, giving them the halo of prestige of speaking at INBOUND and having additional featured content shared with the INBOUND audience, and INBOUND reaps the benefits of the speakers sharing INBOUND content throughout the year.

Slides and event photos are turned into carousels for LinkedIn, fireside chats become quote tiles on Instagram, and video snippets from the event are shared on TikTok and Facebook. The conference powers a year of content for the HubSpot brand and for speakers. And, of course, in-person attendees and digital-pass holders benefit from seeing recaps and following their favorite speakers, and the social media, newsletter, and blog audiences of the INBOUND channels learn more about the conference and the HubSpot brand.

HubSpot introduced the Inbound methodology many years ago, and they've turned their content marketing expertise into a powerhouse brand-, content-, and revenue-accelerator via their official INBOUND conference.

Conclusion

With proper planning, marketers can extend the shelf life of each asset. They need to shape the content early in the creation process to make it easy to create modular content. This means they need to consider the content depth and intent, as well as the asset type and distribution channels, over multiple time horizons.

Chapter Summary

- Modular content allows marketers to create and repurpose assets in multiple ways, going beyond simply cutting short excerpts from a longer asset.
- For maximum reach, engagement, and conversion, marketers should use a mix of decomposition and building blocks to create modular content.

- Assets do not need to stay in their original format or length, and can be trimmed, combined, or reimagined, based on the audience intent, substance, and distribution channel best practices.

- Content should be shaped at the beginning of the creation process to ensure it's suitable for long-tail distribution and can avoid common pitfalls that make it more difficult to mix and match assets and channels.

Notes

1 Duarte, N. (2015) *The Non-Comedian's Guide to Making Jokes in Presentations*, LinkedIn, July 30. linkedin.com/pulse/ha-lessons-embracing-funny-nancy-duarte/? (archived at https://perma.cc/FTS9-AC6L)

2 Duarte, N. and Sanchez, P. (2016) *Illuminate: Ignite Change Through Speeches, Stories, Ceremonies, and Symbols*, Portfolio

Metrics: From Owned to Omni-Channel

05

First Principles of Omni-Channel Metrics

Too many marketers focus on driving short-term, easy-to-measure metrics. This results in a journey that prioritizes owned channels and last-touch attribution models, instead of taking a holistic approach to the modern journey that traverses many channels and touchpoints. To measure impact throughout the playground journey, marketers need to match metrics to the assets and channels that the audience prefers to consume.

If we reject the funnel as the primary model for mapping content, we must also adjust our metrics to match the modern journey, which functions more like a playground.

Technology innovation in the early 2000s heavily impacted how marketers think about measuring marketing activities, attributing deals and revenue to each touchpoint, and overall marketing strategy and tactics. The ability to capture user information with easy-to-create forms, place tracking pixels or cookies on a website session, and store large amounts of data about customers meant that marketers started trying to collect as much information about their audience as possible.

Unfortunately, the bulk of these capabilities are only available on properties controlled by the company, such as the brand website. This means that the marketing strategy shifted from providing information in the most consumable way for the audience, to focusing on capturing visitor information through asset downloads or tracking pixels. The focus on ease-of-tracking also resulted in a bigger shift to prioritize digital channels, instead of considering all available channels, including offline outlets like in-person events, print media, and out-of-home placements.

But audiences are savvy, and often circumvent the tracking through ad blockers or finding the information without needing to provide an email address. Regulations are catching up to improve privacy and security both online and offline, making it more difficult for marketers to easily add tracking capabilities to every touchpoint. And platforms have changed how they show content, often deprioritizing content that takes users off the platform.

All of this resulted in some key shifts for marketing measurement and attribution:

- From using last-touch attribution to multi-touch attribution
- From valuing primarily owned properties and channels to valuing all touchpoints
- From driving referral traffic to driving in-feed or on-platform engagement
- From prioritizing the click-through rate (CTR) to assigning metrics for channel- and asset-specific conversions.

The first principles of omni-channel metrics go back to the first principles of trust: It's about the humans. To focus on the humans traversing a playground journey, we need to agree on the following principles:

- What is easiest to track is not necessarily the best metric to track.
- Goodhart's Law: When the measure becomes a goal, it ceases to be a good measure.[1]
- Building the long-term relationship is more important than capturing a data point or driving a short-term metric.

As we think about how best to measure our marketing efforts, we need to think about which actions we want the humans to take. We must match our metrics to their journey and intent at each step, take a holistic approach to measurement, and understand which tradeoffs we're making throughout the journey by optimizing for different metrics.

From Last-Touch on Owned Properties to Multi-Touch Across All Platforms

First, we need to think beyond last-touch attribution. Last-touch attribution puts all of the weight on the final touch in the journey before a conversion, and thus, overly weights the influence of owned properties on conversions to a buying action (contacting Sales, signing up for the product, or starting a free trial).

Of course, the company website is often the last place a prospect visits before converting, particularly for e-commerce or SaaS companies, where the website is the primary place to buy. And, it's easy to measure, since it's a direct action on an owned property. As we've noted, however, the journey takes many twists and turns, and as marketers, we need to deliver messages in the right place, at the right time, no matter where the audience is in the metaphorical playground.

We can *no longer focus solely on the easiest-to-measure touchpoints in the audience journey*, forcing people to log in, click, or register, simply because it's easier for us to track. Practically, this means giving equal weight to a video view on social media, YouTube, a company landing page, and/or an event microsite. It means finding ways to measure content views shared via personal LinkedIn profiles, company blogs, and event sites, instead of focusing only on referral traffic or CTR from these platforms to the company website.

This is also imperative as more distribution channels become available, and third-party platforms increasingly become pay-to-play. Platforms are greedy, and people are lazy. LinkedIn wants you to stay on LinkedIn. Instagram wants you to stay on Instagram. TikTok wants you to stay on TikTok. Thus, many of these distribution platforms penalize content that's meant to take you to another platform. They impose a link "penalty," reducing the reach of content that includes external links. To overcome this, brands are forced to spend money to buy the same reach that they used to obtain organically, or find creative ways to work around the algorithms if they want to include a link to an owned property.

The audience has a low tolerance for multiple clicks to consume the content they're looking for. They want to see the value right on the platform, instead of needing to go to another site or landing page to read or watch the content.

Omni-Channel Metrics

As we have noted throughout this book, people trust people like themselves. They want to consume content from their favorite creators, influencers, and subject-matter experts. They're more willing to follow an individual compared to a brand handle. Consider the 2024 numbers for these well-known companies and their leaders:

- The Autodesk LinkedIn company page has over 800,000 followers.[2] CMO Dara Treseder has over 125,000 followers on her personal LinkedIn page,[3] and CEO Andrew Anagost has over 20,000 followers,[4] but both frequently receive more reactions and comments than the company page.

- The official Virgin brand account on X has over 240,000 followers,[5] while founder Richard Branson has over 12 million followers on the platform.[6] The Virgin brand portfolio includes music, aviation, health and wellness, and even space ventures, yet Richard Branson continues to be the biggest name in the portfolio.

- Microsoft CEO Satya Nadella's 11 million followers on LinkedIn[7] rival the company page's 25 million followers.[8] That's one executive compared to an entire company with decades of brand equity.

- The official Spanx Instagram account has over 950,000 followers,[9] and founder Sara Blakely is close behind, with over 890,000 followers.[10]

All of these factors mean that brands increasingly need to show the humans behind the screen and allow individuals to distribute content. This goes beyond founders and executives. Leaders can loom large, especially if they found a company that becomes a household name. But, if you consider all the smart, capable employees who work at these brands as potential creators, you understand that empowering them to share enables the company to extend its message, build relationships, and engage with the audience at scale.

Naturally, this makes it more difficult to track, since the marketing team no longer has complete control over every touchpoint. It's hard to bring thousands of data points into a single, unified view, and each channel offers slightly different definitions for many metrics. Consider impressions, views, and entrances. Some platforms consider an "impression" to be any post appearing in someone's feed, even if they scroll past it quickly. Other platforms might consider that to be a "view," or might use the term to indicate that someone dwelled on the content for a longer amount of time (for example, many video "views" require three seconds of time to be counted in this metric). "Entrances" generally refer to organic entrances on a website, usually achieved after someone clicks on a link in the SERP, but it can also be used as a shorthand for any entrance, including those resulting from a referral from an external site, a referral from an internal site, or traffic from emails, ads, or other promotional efforts.

In addition to struggling with standardized definitions, the scale of expected reach or "good" reach is often quite disparate between channels, making it difficult to compare impressions, views, and entrances across channels. If a brand is just starting to build in a channel, it's likely to have significantly fewer impressions than someone more established. If the company pays to drive traffic to a specific channel or asset, the impressions might be several orders of magnitude more than unpaid results. Thus, comparing 10,000 impressions between channels, paid and unpaid campaigns, or industry benchmarks requires more context to understand whether this reach is above average, on target with expectations, or below average.

Fortunately, continued technology improvement now enables marketers to track metrics across multiple channels. Tools such as marketing automation platforms (MAP) have grown in popularity since the early 2010s, and more advanced customer data platforms (CDP) are on the rise since the early 2020s. Incumbents in the MAP category include HubSpot and Marketo, with newcomers like Tealium and Dreamdata gaining traction in the CDP space.

Platform-specific trackers allow marketers to aggregate metrics across non-branded accounts. For example, Shield enables individuals to connect their personal LinkedIn profiles to a unified dashboard, so that teams can review reach, reaction, and comment information across a variety of profiles. This is useful for small-scale employee advocacy or evangelism programs, where distribution via personal accounts is a key part of the overall distribution strategy.

For general tracking, urchin tracking modules (UTMs) help marketers understand more granular elements, including source, medium, campaign, term, and/or content. UTM codes allow teams to understand which channels and campaigns drive traffic and conversions, and allow them to customize links if they're working with influencers, partners, or paid channels.

As we take a holistic view of distribution on a journey that behaves like a playground, we must also choose a primary metric to optimize for each asset and each channel. For example, it's unlikely that we can optimize for in-feed engagement, like positive comments on social media, and *also* drive a significant CTR on the same post. Do we want the individual to engage or click?

MEASURING THOUGHT LEADERSHIP ACTIVITIES

The struggle between measuring short-term, trackable conversion or long-term affinity and engagement comes up often when discussing thought leadership activities. We know we need to share a unique point of view, shape the conversation, and help our audience think differently about problems and solutions. But this takes time, and the mindset shift is difficult to measure. How do we know if we're increasing trust, rapport, and affinity with our audience by sharing thought leadership content?

Many marketers try to force these activities to fit into the same buy-intent box, using forms to gate content, and then measuring the number of downloads, or scoring this content consumption as a marketing-qualified lead (MQL). Others try to insert buy-intent CTAs into thought leadership content, resulting in low levels of conversion because the intention of the audience is mismatched to the content. Most thought leadership content sits at the conceptual or strategic depth, with a trust or learn intent. Thus, tossing in a CTA to purchase the company's offering is out of place.

Instead, consider specific metrics for thought leadership activities, including:

- Citations, references, and/or backlinks to your thought leadership content. For example, if you publish original research, how often is that research mentioned by other practitioners?
- Inbound invitations to be a podcast guest, conference speaker, and/or byline contributor for relevant outlets
- Shares or reposts of thought leadership content on social media sites
- Increase in brand recall and/or net promoter score in brand surveys after investing in thought leadership activities.

We must also consider time horizons in our metrics. If someone is entering the playground for the first time, they're probably going to take a quick look around to understand what's available. This means that if you immediately force them to choose the slide or the swings, they might just exit the playground, instead of making a choice.

The same is true for our audience. Forcing them down a buy-intent path upon first engagement is likely to result in an exit. Thus, we should match metrics with the intent. As we discussed in Chapter 3 on playground elements, key intents include trust, buy, use, help, and learn. For example, a general search for the basics of a topic is unlikely to indicate buying intent. Thus, the metrics might focus on SERP position and entrances rather than a buy-intent conversion. In contrast, if someone searches "Top five tools for [problem you solve]," they are much more likely to be interested in actually trying a product, and conversion metrics such as starting a free trial or requesting a demo are appropriate.

This means marketing teams must be aligned with the sales teams, and, where relevant, their customer success or delivery teams. Understanding metrics like the average sales cycle, deal velocity, and time to value helps marketers create leading and lagging indicators throughout the audience journey.

Too often, marketers focus on time horizons that are too short compared to the sales cycle or historical benchmarks. To combat this, we have created metrics that attempt to show progress through the linear funnel, including MQLs (marketing-qualified leads) and SQLs (sales-qualified leads). These are achieved through complicated scoring models, based primarily on owned touchpoints. For example, consider that someone visits a company web page that includes a form to fill out to access an asset. By filling out the form, they receive a certain number of points. Because they provided their email address in the form, they're added to an email nurture campaign. Each email opened or clicked results in additional points. After reaching the prescribed points threshold, a sales representative contacts the person to try to book a meeting.

But all of these metrics ignore the touchpoints that the person experienced before landing on the company website! By basing the marketing goals on metrics like MQLs per quarter, teams focus only on the short-term, buy-intent conversion. This results in underinvesting in long-term strategy and the tactics to build trust and affinity, well before a person is ready, willing, and able to buy.

As we saw in Chapter 3 on elements in the playground, explicit CTAs result in understanding explicit audience intent. When we think about metrics like MQLs, we need to refine what they mean in order to match the intent. In the past, we defined an MQL as marketers deciding to score any action that represents engagement via an owned distribution channel, and upon reaching the scoring threshold, considering this person a "lead." In the playground we define an MQL as someone who has taken an explicit, buy-intent action. So, for example:

- Book a demo = MQL
- Contact sales = MQL
- Start a trial = MQL.

We can also see negative effects of misaligned intent by looking at metrics like email unsubscribe rates and low retention or view-through rates on videos or webinars. These actions indicate that we haven't met the audience's need with our content.

Lack of engagement and slowing follower growth are negative indicators that the content is not resonating with your audience on social media, while reduced reach might indicate that you're not creating and sharing according to the algorithm requirements or best practices for individual platforms.

Matching Assets, Channels, Intent, and Metrics

As we have seen in previous chapters, we need to match the substance of our content to the right formats and channels. We must do the same for our metrics. For example, learn-intent content and buy-intent content should not use the same metrics for success—because the intent is completely different. The audience's actions resulting from consuming learn-intent content versus buy-intent content are different, and attempting to force the audience to take buy-intent actions from learn-intent content results in poor performance against the metrics for the marketing team, and a poor experience for the audience.

Instead, we want to match our metrics to the intent, asset, and channel. We know this intuitively: We can't measure "average minutes watched" for content that does not include a video. We might consider a similar metric, like "dwell time" or "scroll depth" for articles and landing pages, but it's not a one-to-one metric that we use for video. We also understand that people are unlikely to make a purchase from a non-company-owned site in the B2B world. Online retailers such as Amazon and Shopify have built trust and brand awareness over the years to entice buyers to purchase from their storefronts, but higher-risk, complex deals also happen via company-owned properties, and generally require someone to connect with a sales representative from the company to finalize the contract. This means that we can't use conversion metrics for CTAs like "sign up" or "buy now" directly from a third-party site because the person will need an interim touchpoint on an owned property (this could be the company website, or connecting with a solution partner or sales representative).

Instead, we consider leading metrics like entrances, impressions, followers, engagement (reactions, comments, shares, profile views), profile tags, hashtag usage, CTR, and referral traffic for these channels. We must also understand that these are not "vanity" metrics and can be an end in themselves. For example, contributed articles to a top industry publication are trust-intent content, which is a precursor to buying behavior. Such articles also offer additional benefits for brand awareness, which might attract job candidates, bolster confidence from investors, and create partnership opportunities. In this case, the primary metrics might be article views and references or backlinks within a specified period of time.

EXAMPLES OF QUANTITATIVE METRICS, MATCHED TO INTENT

People often ask which metrics match each intent. The following list is not comprehensive and will continue to evolve as new channels and asset types become available, but it's helpful to see tactical examples of quantitative metrics to use for each intent.

Trust-Intent

Leading Indicators

- Shares of an asset on social media
- Views or impressions
- Consumption rate, average watch time, view-through or retention rate
- Press coverage (for example when releasing a report or original research)

Lagging Indicators

- References, citations, and backlinks
- Tags of an employee or at-mentions of the company
- Inbound invitations to publish or speak
- Increase in prestige of outlets (such as an invitation to present the keynote speech versus a breakout session at a conference, or the ability to publish in a high-profile industry publication)

Buy-Intent

Leading Indicators

- Request to contact Sales or meetings booked

- Account sign-ups
- Activating a free trial
- Demo request
- Request for proposal (RFP)—inclusion in the RFP, RFPs closed and won or closed and lost

Lagging Indicators

- Upgrade to a higher service tier or premium product edition, account expansion, contract renewal
- Customer testimonials or referrals
- Discount code redemption
- Reduced churn rate (products or subscriptions) or cancellation rate (services)

Use-Intent

Leading Indicators

- Taking the action specified in the content (such as activating a template after consuming the onboarding material that includes a template recommendation)
- Demo or tutorial views
- High placement in SERPs for queries related to your offering

Lagging Indicators

- Feature utilization
- Active users (daily, weekly, or monthly) and product activation (creating a project, making a dashboard, implementing a template, adding users or data)
- Inviting a teammate into the product
- Agreeing to share a testimonial, case study, or reference
- User-generated content (UGC) on social media or community forums
- Organic entrances to documentation, tutorials, or guides
- Net promoter score (NPS), customer effort score (CES), customer satisfaction (CSAT)

- Reduced churn rate (products or subscriptions) or cancellation rate (services)
- Office hours or monthly account meetings (show rate versus cancellation rate, ad hoc booking requests, response rate to emails from the account representative or customer success team)

Help-Intent

Leading Indicators

- Entrances to documentation or help center, either organic or via referral traffic
- Entrances to community forums
- Lower bounce rates (for example if someone encounters an error, but support documentation helps them fix the problem to continue their journey)

Lagging Indicators

- Support tickets (reduced quantity, reduced time to resolution)
- NPS, CES, CSAT

Learn-Intent

Leading Indicators

- Rankings for specific keywords, SERP placements
- Shares on social media
- Entrances, views, and impressions
- Email sign-ups, open-rate, and CTR (for example on a monthly email newsletter)
- Consumption rate, average watch time, view-through, or retention rate on videos
- Scroll depth of written content

Lagging Indicators

- Follower growth, increased in-feed engagement
- Backlinks or reference links
- Citations in podcasts, conference presentations, and/or books

These metrics should be measured consistently over time to understand trends such as seasonality, channel health, and business impact. These should also be combined with qualitative metrics to understand how audiences perceive and engage with the brand.

Balancing Quantitative and Qualitative Metrics

While digital channels like social media, websites, and advertising are easier to track for both positive and negative metrics, offline channels are increasingly important, as audiences are inundated with more content and more channels.

In-person events offer an opportunity for humans to connect directly with other humans. These gatherings allow us to shake hands, share meals, and exchange information in real time. They're also an opportunity to gain qualitative and quantitative data in real time.

For example, many teams focus on scanning badges for every attendee who comes to their booth. These scans are scored to contribute to the MQLs from the event and contribute to the overall success metrics in post-event analysis. Yet, we have real-time data about the foot traffic to the booth. We can see if it's busy compared to competitors. Using my provocative approach to offer a giveaway, demos, or simply being helpful, we get a sense of whether our ideal customers are attending the event. We get an idea of whether the message resonates because we can see how long people stay in the booth having conversations. Similarly, if you have someone speaking at the event, you can gauge interest in the topic or speaker by how full the session room is. If speakers from your company deliver sessions at events throughout the year, you can compare the popularity of the speaker and the topics they share. Hosting a happy hour or dinner during a larger conference is another popular tactic to deepen relationships with a subset of attendees. How many people RSVP to attend your side events? What is the show rate? How long do people stay at the happy hour or dinner? These quantitative metrics give you a sense of the initial popularity of your offering, and qualitative metrics give you a sense for whether it resonates with the audience in attendance.

You can connect these offline metrics to online metrics. For example, did attendees share pictures of your booth or giveaway? Did they post takeaways from your session on social media? Did they use a branded hashtag or at-mention the brand handles?

REAL-WORLD EXAMPLE   Palerra Exhibits at AWS re:Invent

Let's take a look at how a real-world company approached the journey with a playground mindset and united its online and offline metrics.

Palerra is a cloud access security broker, acquired by Oracle in 2016. Its flagship product helps users detect and remediate security issues in cloud-based software applications.[11]

The team sponsored a booth at AWS re:Invent, a popular industry conference that attracts tens of thousands of attendees each year. In order to stand out with a smaller booth, the team decided to take a creative approach to the booth giveaway. They placed an Amazon Tap device inside a clear, locked case. They placed a bowl of what looked like identical keys next to the case. If an attendee drew a key and unlocked the case, they won the Tap.

Naturally, many attendees were skeptical that there were any working keys in the bowl. So, every time someone unlocked the case and removed the Amazon Tap, the team asked to take a picture to share on the company Twitter handle. They tagged the winner, who often reshared the post, showcasing their prize. They invited anyone who stopped by the booth to follow the company social media account to see how often someone won, and showed the social media feed with winners' pictures to attendees who voiced concerns about drawing a key from the bowl.

In exchange for watching a short demo, they offered to let an attendee draw additional keys to try their luck at unlocking the case. They connected the giveaway to the demo by showing use cases involving the digital security keys included with cloud products, and asking questions like, "Who has access to the keys?" and, "What happens to the keys when they are no longer needed?"

The team also created a book of *AWS Cautionary Tales*, telling customer stories of security vulnerabilities the product detected and helped fix. They offered the book as a hard copy at the booth and online as a PDF. They gave conference attendees the option to take a physical book with them, or have it emailed to them after the event. Many attendees requested the email, since they didn't want to carry more literature around the show floor. This gave the team a substantial reason to follow up with people whose badges were scanned, which increased the open-rates and CTRs of the post-event email, since attendees had a more memorable experience at the booth.

The team also used the digital version of the book to engage social media followers who were not attending the conference. Along with pictures of giveaway winners, they sprinkled in stories from the book and linked out to the full PDF for more details.

How did the team measure the success of their activities at re:Invent that year? They used a mix of real-time, qualitative information and post-event digital touchpoints. They observed that the booth was busier than surrounding booths during the opening reception. They saw an increase in badge scans at the booth, along with increased engagement in post-event follow-ups via email campaigns and personalized sales outreach. They saw an increase in followers and engagement on the company social media handles. And they saw an increase in views of the digital version of the *Cautionary Tales* book in the 30 days following the event.

Of course, some of the people they talked to at the event were or became customers, but that success can't be attributed to this single touchpoint or set of touchpoints. It requires the marketing team to connect with the sales and customer success teams to get the right people in the room at the event, and tailor the follow-up to engage attendees after the event.

Events are not the only channel to balance quantitative and qualitative metrics. Collecting feedback in digital channels might also result in qualitative insights. For example, sentiment analysis via listening tools on social media helps the marketing team understand what audiences are saying about the brand and offerings. This type of analysis looks at the language used instead of focusing on traditional metrics like reach and engagement. Alternatively, qualitative feedback on the website—which might include questions about how to buy from the company, which verticals a brand serves, or the top challenges the offering solves—can help the team understand where they might have gaps in information, where the message is unclear, or where there are navigational issues on the company website.

REAL-WORLD EXAMPLE   Digital Detox in Vienna

The city of Vienna wanted to increase tourism to the city and to Austria, and decided to run a unique, counterintuitive campaign. The tagline? *Enjoy Vienna, not #Vienna. Unhashtag your vacation!*

That's right: It specifically told visitors *not* to post pictures on social media with the hashtag of the city name. It didn't want people focused on taking pictures with the perfect location, framing, and lighting. It didn't want people glued to their phones, posting about their perfect vacation. Instead, visitors were invited to pick up an instant camera at the local tourist center upon arriving in Vienna, with the recommendation of taking only 10 pictures for the whole trip, using the analog camera to capture the experience. Can you imagine taking an international trip and only snapping a handful of pictures on a non-digital camera?

The city also created a website, showcasing curated itineraries based on themed interests. For example, one itinerary featured local wineries, breweries, and artisan food makers, tailored for visitors who like to taste craft cocktails and cuisine. Another itinerary offered details about local trails, gardens, and parks for the outdoors enthusiasts. They featured local businesses and made it easy for visitors to choose an itinerary based on length of stay, interests, and accommodations.

The messaging was tied to overall health and well-being, touting the benefits of a digital detox, along with signs for the audience that it might be time to pursue a digital detox. The team invited influencers to enjoy the city without focusing on posting loads of pictures, reels, or vlogs. It featured photos from their instant cameras on the website, with a section for "influencers on digital detox."

To promote Vienna as a vacation destination, the team ran out-of-home campaigns in major cities including New York and San Francisco. These are digital hubs, with lots of people posting pictures on social media. So, analog ads in train stations and bus terminals, promoting the idea that you should *not* hashtag Vienna, disrupted the usual barrage of promotions for new apps, websites, and QR codes.

But, how might the city of Vienna measure the success of this campaign? Most marketers focus on brand mentions or branded hashtags to track campaigns on social media. But Vienna specifically chose not to focus on this metric.

Instead, it needed to rely on more traditional, human-centered metrics:

- Increase in requests for tourist visas
- Increase in foot traffic at the tourist office and local businesses
- Figures of how many instant cameras were loaned out and returned
- Increase in revenue for the city and local businesses featured on the website
- Increase in organic searches for "Vienna," "visit Vienna," and "Vienna vacation/holiday," along with more entrances to the campaign website.

As you can see, building meaningful connections that drive revenue is not always easy to track, but it leaves a lasting impression on the audience.

Driving Impact Through Optimization

Which is better: publishing more new content or optimizing existing content? An effective content strategy requires both, but it's a struggle to balance the two tactics, particularly in a resource-constrained environment.

Many teams default to net-new because they're measured on how much or how often they publish (more on the pitfalls of this metric in the next section). It feels great to say that you published lots of new blogs or videos this month. It's easy to understand for stakeholders, easy to measure for creators, and easy to track in dashboards. But, what's the impact? Did you reach a new audience? Did you help an existing audience? What's the quality of the content? Does it convert into whatever next action you wanted to see?

Content optimization is an underutilized tool in the marketer's toolkit to increase content impact. You've probably heard several phrases that allude to this truth, such as: Set it and forget it; out of sight, out of mind; and publish fast, publish often. But, allowing content to languish is not good for the audience or the business.

For example, "freshness" has long been considered a factor for rankings in SERPs. Search engines look for the most up-to-date and accurate information for each query, which leads them to give preference to content with current information and authority. This means that refreshing your content by adding new information and updating the publish date, augmenting content by adding media elements, and staying current with trends like featured snippets and summaries, helps your content stay towards the top of the SERPs.

I experienced this myself, falling into the "publish more" trap. I was churning, churning, churning to get new content out the door in tandem with a big launch announcement. Yes, we needed that content, but our impact suffered because of this net-new-only focus. When we finally took a step back to dig into the data to see what was working, what needed immediate improvement, and how to double down on the right things, we saw a significant improvement in our rankings, entrances, and sign-up metrics. Our optimization yielded more impact.

It's not just my little corner of the business in this one instance. We see "debt" from years of defaulting to net-new. This is how you end up with cluttered sites, outdated content, and orphan pages that don't serve you or the audience.

Consider these elements for your next optimization project:

- Cross-linking to owned content
- Updating or adding screenshots
- Updating or adding audio or visual media
- Improving H1s, H2s, and featured snippets or summaries
- Sunsetting or archiving outdated or underperforming content
- Adding transcripts to audio or visual media
- Updating or adding descriptions or alt-text to your images (beneficial for accessibility and SEO).

As you think about increasing the impact of your content, build optimization rituals to ensure you're getting the most out of existing content before creating a net-new asset.

Beyond Attribution: Content Velocity

We've talked a lot about measuring the impact of content for business goals and thinking about if and how much our content attracts, engages, and converts the right audience. But, we haven't talked about metrics for the internal team.

Unfortunately, many teams have goals related to content quantity and, by extension, speed. Write 10 blog posts per month, publish three videos per quarter, upload seven PDFs to the sales asset hub… These quantity metrics don't account for quality, and they don't properly reflect the true cost of content creation and distribution, or the downstream impact of the content. This is particularly troublesome if leadership expects or "counts" only net-new content.

As we discussed in Chapter 4 on increasing reach, conversion, and engagement, modular content allows marketers to extend the shelf life, reach, and impact of each asset by decomposing large assets into smaller elements or combining short assets into long-form content. It allows them to meet the audience in the right place with the right content, since some people prefer videos on social media, others like to read long-form articles on their favorite publishing site, and others enjoy listening to podcasts on their morning commute. Do these assets deserve to be counted as having less quantity or requiring less effort, simply because they're not "new"?

This mindset also results in misaligned incentives and unclear definitions of what "counts" as "content." As more and more platforms encourage users to share and consume shorter content, more frequently, "content" might be multiple social media posts in a single day. Do we count each post in a thread on Instagram or X as an individual piece of "content"?

In other cases, "more" content not only has diminishing returns, it might also be counterproductive. In the previous section, we discussed content optimization. This becomes even more important in the age of AI, when tools can churn out hundreds of articles or pages in a matter of minutes or hours. Unfortunately, some teams have started using AI tools to create massive amounts of content to fuel their SEO programs. This creates problems with duplicative content, and Google has started penalizing this low-quality content in the SERPs. So, not only are they wasting time and money to publish more articles, they're also damaging their domain authority due to penalties for low-quality content.

As you can see, not only does "more" not necessarily mean "better," it can even have negative impacts. Instead, I recommend using a different metric—**content velocity**. Content velocity is about accelerating the time to value of creating modular content from a pillar asset or combining multiple small assets into a larger asset. This is a perfect use case for incorporating AI into your workflows and understanding how this impacts the quantity and quality of the assets you create.

For example, I've been experimenting with tools to generate short video clips from longer video assets. Do we end up with more videos? Maybe, but it depends on the quality of the content. The AI tool spits out between 5 and 25 clips, and then a human on my team goes through and chooses the three to five clips that are suitable for distribution. As part of our internal delivery process, we mark which channels the clip is relevant for, note personas and products mentioned in each clip, recommend relevant existing articles for cross-linking or embedding the videos, and suggest CTAs and destinations for each CTA. This package of clips is much more strategic than simply passing along the 25 AI-generated clips to our campaign teams.

Yes, 25 is more than 3. But the *right* three messages, with information about the *right* audience and *right* channels mean significantly higher quality, with a higher likelihood of being usable for our distribution teams, and resonating with our audience.

So, content velocity helps you understand how fast you can achieve the *right* "more" content because velocity is not just about speed, but speed in the right direction. Indicators associated with content velocity include cycle time, number of channels used, and references.

Cycle time is determined by how long it takes to produce the required asset from start to finish. The team agrees on the trigger to start the project and the activity to complete the project. For example, the trigger to start might be receiving the request or accessing a source file, and the completion might be uploading the project to a central asset repository for other teams to access.

The **number of channels used** indicates the usefulness of an asset. For example, a single short product demo video might be shared as a native upload on a social media channel from the brand handle and a personal handle, embedded into a related article, used as part of the onboarding materials for a new product, and included in the support documentation for the product. That's five different channels for a single asset! Marketers need to be careful using this metric, because it's possible to improve it simply by distributing the asset in every channel. As we'll discuss in Chapters 6 and 7, on the social media spectrum and the new rules of social media, we need to tailor our assets to match the algorithm rules and audience consumption preferences in each channel.

And finally, **references** are measured by how often the asset is linked to or cited in other places. This is particularly relevant for large pillar assets, such as annual surveys, trends reports, and original research. Creating a social media carousel of key statistics from the report and linking to the full report counts as a reference. Writing a blog post to serve as an overview of the findings and linking to the full report counts as a reference. How often is the report sent out after a sales call or in-person event? Again, the goal is to help the team measure whether the up-front investment yields additional content to fuel programs and campaigns.

Combining content velocity with the optimization metrics noted earlier in the chapter allows marketers to show that they're not only working hard, but smart. They're serving the audience with the right messages, in the right channels, in the right formats.

Conclusion

As we think about building a playground to create a seamless, helpful, and impactful audience journey, we must shift our approach to measurement and attribution to reflect all the activities and touchpoints.

We can no longer focus simply on metrics that are easy to track on digital, owned properties. Instead, we need to consider both quantitative and qualitative metrics, matching assets, channels, and intent in a way that prioritizes the audience experience.

This means that we optimize to deliver value where the audience spends time, instead of trying to force them to an owned property. It means that we take a holistic approach to measurement, including real-time metrics in person—like a busy booth or well-attended conference talk—not just the click-through rate or referral traffic from one digital channel to another.

And we recognize that creating net-new content might not be the highest return on investment. Incorporating optimization and modular content creation into our timelines and metrics helps us improve the audience journey, as well as efficiency, impact, and ROI.

Chapter Summary

- Traditional metrics like CTR and MQLs force marketing teams to prioritize ease of tracking over the audience experience. Instead, marketers need to take a holistic approach that mirrors the audience journey through a playground.

- Move beyond last-touch attribution that prioritizes owned properties and forces people into a buy-intent journey too early. Instead, match channels and assets with audience intent.

- Consider how optimization and content velocity impact your choice of metrics. More content is not necessarily better, and extending the reach, engagement, and impact of each asset helps increase ROI and improve the audience experience.

Notes

1 Goodhart, C. (1975) Problems of Monetary Management: The U.K. Experience, *Papers in Monetary Economics, 1975*, Vol. 1, pp. 1–20, Reserve Bank of Australia

2 Autodesk (2025) Follower count, LinkedIn, January, linkedin.com/company/autodesk (archived at https://perma.cc/M4ZD-4VG7)

3 Treseder, D. (2025) Follower count, LinkedIn, January, linkedin.com/in/daratreseder (archived at https://perma.cc/4CK4-JYWJ)

4 Anagnost, A. (2025) Follower count, LinkedIn, January, linkedin.com/in/andrewanagnost (archived at https://perma.cc/LZZ6-2HNC)

5 Virgin (2025) Follower count, X, January, x.com/virgin (archived at https://perma.cc/E8ER-6FTR)

6 Branson, R. (2025) Follower count, X, January, x.com/richardbranson (archived at https://perma.cc/NE3H-7XMG)

7   Nadella, S. (2025) Follower count, LinkedIn, January, linkedin.com/in/satyanadella (archived at https://perma.cc/2XA8-856N)

8   Microsoft (2025) Follower count, LinkedIn, January, linkedin.com/company/microsoft (archived at https://perma.cc/LCE8-N45F)

9   Spanx (2025) Follower count, Instagram, January, instagram.com/spanx (archived at https://perma.cc/V8M4-EX89)

10 Blakely, S. (2025) Follower count, Instagram, January, instagram.com/sarablakely (archived at https://perma.cc/VNS6-FB6B)

11 Kurand, S. (2016) Oracle Acquires Cloud Access Security Brokerage Startup Palerra, CRN, September 19, crn.com/news/security/300082128/oracle-acquires-cloud-access-security-brokerage-startup-palerra?itc=refresh (archived at https://perma.cc/28QA-8FCN)

The Social Media Spectrum

06

Beyond Distribution

Social media has evolved from a place to post company news and job requisitions to a robust set of channels and tactics to connect with multiple audiences. The social media spectrum helps marketers assess and improve their efforts to identify and engage their audience in the right place. By moving from communication, to conversation, to community, brands can build deep relationships with their audience, at scale.

As we saw in Chapter 5, many founders and executives have a following on social media that is greater than or equal to the following of their brand handles. And, as we saw in the opening chapter on trust, people trust people like themselves. So, it makes sense that audiences gravitate towards individuals, rather than the brand.

Surely this means that we should ditch brand handles and focus solely on individual profiles? Unfortunately, it's not as straightforward as simply elevating executive or employee handles. Instead, we need to think about the trade-offs of the relationships, goals, and key metrics between brand accounts and individual accounts.

Key Areas Along the Social Media Spectrum

Whether you're focused on building accounts for the brand or elevating employees' accounts, you must consider where you are on the *social media spectrum* (Figure 6.1).

Figure 6.1   Social Media Spectrum

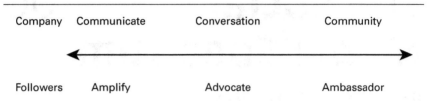

The social media spectrum consists of three key areas for the brand page or profile: Communication, Conversation, and Community, with three key coordinating areas for followers: Amplify, Advocate, and Ambassador.

Let's break each one down by looking at the common definition of each word, starting with brands looking to communicate and hoping their followers will amplify. The common definition of "communicate" is a one-way sharing of ideas, information, or news. For brands in this phase, social media is a means to broadcast their information: "We've won an award," "We're hosting a webinar," "We're announcing a new product." They're primarily focused on communicating their message. We generally define "amplify" as increasing the volume. In this case, brands want followers to make their message louder. They want followers and employees to increase the reach of their message by sharing the content.

In the next stage of the social media spectrum is the conversation/advocate pairing. The widely used definition of "conversation" is an informal talk between two or more people, where they share news and exchange ideas. This generally means that brands are trying to enter or start a conversation and want to feel that there's a two-way exchange between the brand handle and the followers. In this case, brands want their followers to be advocates, commonly defined as individuals who publicly recommend or support a company, person, or concept.

Finally, on the far end of the spectrum, is the community/ambassador pairing. "Community" is generally defined as a feeling of connection in a group, based on shared goals, common interests, and similar attitudes and outlook. An "ambassador" is often someone who acts as a representative or promoter of a specific idea or activity.

This is a marked difference between the two previously mentioned phases, as the brand is not taking the spotlight.

You'll notice some specific differentiation between the definitions, particularly when we apply them to brands engaging on social media.

The communicate/amplify stage of the social media spectrum is highly focused on the brand needs and goals. The brand communicates information and asks followers to "make it louder" by increasing the reach through sharing, reacting, and commenting. This is an outdated approach to social media, using it solely as a broadcast mechanism or distribution channel.

In contrast, the conversation/advocate phase recognizes that brands need to create a relationship with their followers, but still puts the brand at the center. It's about hosting or driving the discussion, encouraging participants to engage directly with the brand, and generally centering the conversation on brand-related topics. In this case, the brand wants its followers and employees to show up on its behalf by bringing up sanctioned talking points, inviting the brand into the conversation officially, and defending the brand against naysayers.

In the third phase, community/ambassador, we see a significant shift away from the brand as the hero or driver. Instead, we see the brand as a participant. It's engaging in spaces where the conversation is already flourishing and making space for others to join and engage. In this phase, the brand wants its followers to be ambassadors, uniting people around relevant topics, pain-points, solutions, and, where relevant, the brand.

Tactics and Metrics in Each Phase of the Social Media Spectrum

Brands need to use a mix of all three styles on the spectrum to be successful, but they should not rely too heavily on the communicate/amplify end of the spectrum. Instead, brands should focus most of their efforts on the conversation/advocate and community/ambassador stages of the spectrum.

This is because these two phases focus on two-way or multi-way conversations, building rapport and trust with the audience, and exchanging value in multiple ways. So, how does a brand know which end of the spectrum it's on? How does a brand measure the activities in each phase of the spectrum? Let's look at each phase.

Communicate and Amplify: CTR and Referral Traffic

In the communicate/amplify phase, brands treat each social media platform as a distribution channel. They post links to other sites, with a particular focus on owned properties, such as the company blog, product tour, or campaign landing pages.

Post tactics tend to read like announcements:

- We're hosting a webinar.
- We won an award!
- We've launched a new feature.

As you can see, the primary tone is "we." What we as a brand care about. Find out more about us as a brand. In this case, the primary metrics are click-through rate (CTR) and entrances or referral traffic from social media, since all of the actual substance of the content exists outside of the social media post.

The brand is focused on optimizing the number of people who click a link from a social media channel to an owned property. These metrics are easy to track, since the information is available on properties controlled by the brand. The CTR metrics are available either in the native dashboard for the brand handle or page or in an aggregate social media management tool dashboard, like Sprout Social or Hootsuite. It's simple to put tracking pixels on your own sites, and most out-of-the-box dashboard tools make it easy to see entrances and referral traffic, allowing you to see the traffic coming from both the brand handle and followers amplifying the post by sharing the link on their own channels.

These metrics focus on an extremely short time horizon and compare each post to the best-performing posts. Because most social media content has a short shelf life, the CTRs tend to get pulled into a monthly report, and only remembered if a post performs significantly above average. Even in that case, leadership might not dig into why it performed so well, but, instead, reset their expectations for how well posts should perform (for example, news that a company acquired another company or the departure of a key executive tend to generate significantly higher CTRs than announcements about events or awards).

Secondary metrics might include follower growth and reach or impressions in the social media feed. Follower growth is easy to track, as this information is displayed publicly on most social media profiles. Unfortunately, the raw number reveals little about the nature or quality of the followers, and the expectation is that the account continues to grow indefinitely.

Reach and impressions can be harder to aggregate, since some social media platforms make it difficult to integrate their analytics into an aggregate dashboard. However, marketers can find this information by logging into each platform natively and creating platform-specific reports.

Unfortunately, platforms are greedy, and people are lazy! The platforms want people to remain on the platform. LinkedIn wants to keep people on LinkedIn, Instagram wants people to stay on Instagram, and so on. Thus, many platforms penalize links that take a viewer to another site.

For example, in 2024, Instagram still won't allow clickable links in a post caption in the feed; instead, it requires you to add the link to your profile page. "Link in bio" is a popular callout on posts in the feed, since you can't click a URL added to a post. Similarly, multiple "hacks" have been shared to thwart the LinkedIn algorithm that reduces the reach on posts that contain links, including adding the URL in the comments, and editing a post to include a link after it gains some engagement.

It's not just platforms that dislike links to content shared elsewhere. Audiences want value right in their feed! They don't want to click a link, open another tab, or download a file. They want to consume the value in the place where they're already spending time. The playground approach to the audience journey recognizes and caters to these preferences.

Marketer Amanda Natividad coined the term "Zero-Click Marketing" to describe this approach.[1] Her definition is exactly what it sounds like: creating content that does not require a click. It means that a post needs to stand on its own, adding value to the consumer, regardless of whether they click a link or a call-to-action to consume more content.

Yes, sometimes brands simply need to communicate information by broadcasting it on social media. It's hard to add depth when a post is meant to inform the audience about a time-bound event or recently released company news. We can't assume though that our audience will click the link, and using CTR and referral traffic or entrances as the primary metrics for social media channels means that brands miss most of the value available in these platforms. Fortunately, many brands have figured out that simply sharing links on social media no longer works, and have moved into the next phase of the spectrum.

Conversation and Advocacy: In-Feed Engagement and Mentions

In the conversation/advocate phase, brands try to find, host, and drive conversations with their audience. These conversations tend to be focused on a small subset of the audience members, and brands hope to focus the conversations on the brand and related topics. The mindset is that the brand is talking *to* its audience, and the audience is talking about the brand.

Post tactics tend to request that people engage:

- At-mention us (@BrandHandle)
- Comment on our post
- Tag another friend to join our thread.

Thus, primary metrics in this phase include in-feed engagement on brand posts and brand-related content, and brand mentions or brand tags. Brand mentions and brand tags happen when an audience member specifically uses the brand name or product name in their content.

The key difference in these metrics is that they're brand-focused. It's about how many people comment on a post on a company page on LinkedIn, how many people at-mention the brand on X, or how many people use a campaign-related hashtag during an event. Everything revolves around the brand name, brand hashtags, and brand terms. These metrics also focus on short-term value for the brand, and often look at month-over-month growth or time-bound campaigns that run for less than a single quarter. In some cases, brands might include engagement with specific employee handles or profiles. Unfortunately, it's usually limited to a few executives, with a specific focus on company news. Metrics in this phase are more difficult to track, since some metrics are public, while others require the marketer to set up tracking separately.

Platforms like LinkedIn, Facebook, and Instagram, for example, show the reactions and comments publicly on each post. X and TikTok also show the views for each post publicly. However, none of these platforms show at-mentions, tags, or hashtag use in the post in their public metrics. Marketers need to set up specific tracking to see this information and may need to export a detailed report natively from the platform. As we discussed in Chapter 5 on metrics, tools like Shield help track individual LinkedIn profiles. Some social media tools, such as Sprout Social or Hootsuite, allow marketers to track specific hashtags and different types of mention, including "dark mentions" where a user names a brand or product, but does not formally tag the official handle.

This is one reason some brands still struggle to move into this phase of the spectrum: It's more difficult to show impact. This is further complicated by the fact that social media platforms measure and share performance indicators in different ways. For example, LinkedIn doesn't currently (early 2025) allow a brand page to engage on a user's post unless the user at-mentions the brand. This means that the brand can see when someone includes its name or uses its hashtag, but it can't react or comment on the post unless it's specifically tagged.

This is where the advocate element of the pairing comes in. Since the brand can't always see or engage on posts, it wants its followers to bring it into conversations. Continuing the LinkedIn example, a brand can mitigate the lack of an initial tag by having someone tag the brand page in the comments.

This tactic is foundational in employee advocacy programs, giving the brand a cohort of people to keep an eye out for relevant conversations in which to tag the brand. For smaller teams, the social media manager might manipulate the system by logging in with their personal social media handle, tagging the brand handle, and then logging in as the brand to engage.

Despite the workarounds, focusing on conversations with and about the brand as a core tactic results in lost opportunities, simply because users might not know that they need to tag the brand in order to have a conversation with that brand. To combat this, many brands default to engaging in conversations that happen on their page or on their posts. They don't attempt to find and engage users who are talking about the brand elsewhere, only engaging with comments, reactions, or direct messages on their own posts. Effectively, they're treating the brand page or handle as an owned property, once again forcing the audience to meet the brand where it is, instead of the brand meeting the audience where they are.

The mindset shift towards truly meeting the audience where they are brings us to the third phase of the spectrum: Community/ambassador.

Community and Ambassador: Sentiment and Multi-Channel Engagement

In the community/ambassador phase, the brand acts as a participant in the broader conversation and encourages or yields the floor to other participants and experts in the space. Instead of trying to force the conversation to focus on the brand, the brand page, employees, customers, partners, and other experts take the lead, talking about industry trends, best practices, and generally related topics in the space. The mindset is that the brand is talking *with* the audience, and the audience is talking about topics that the brand cares about.

The post tactics are very different in this phase, with less focus on what the brand posts, and more on the overall conversation. It's not even about the brand handle or page engaging, and it's not focused primarily on customers or employees engaging explicitly on behalf of the brand. While some brands do host community forums, those spaces are largely populated and moderated by the participants. Employees of the company might share posts or comment, but they're not the core drivers of engagement.

I liken this to hosting a party. If I invited a group of friends and professional contacts to my house for a party, it would be odd to gather them into the living room to listen while I stand and speak at length about myself, my career, and my hobbies. It would also be strange if I interrupted smaller conversations to pontificate about my own interests. No one wants to hang out with someone who only talks about themselves. They want to hang out with people who make them feel cool and smart, and introduce them to other cool, smart people. That's why a good host makes it comfortable for guests to engage with each other. Yes, the host goes around to greet each person, and might join conversations throughout the evening, but the host is not the center of attention or the driver of conversations, and does not force specific topics to be discussed. The host refills the plates and the glasses, makes introductions as guests arrive, and moves from group to group to make sure everyone enjoys themselves.

Brands in the community phase do the same thing, and they hope that their followers act as ambassadors, seamlessly participating in the conversation, and, when relevant or explicitly asked, speaking on behalf of the brand. The brand trusts these people to share insights and direct other people to the best resources when asked, regardless of whether they specifically state that they're a customer, employee, or fan of the brand.

Metrics in this phase are quite difficult to track, since they're not focused on owned properties, either brand pages or handles, or off-platform spaces like blogs and landing pages. Instead, brands in this phase focus on sentiment and multi-channel engagement. Similar to the metrics we saw for learn-intent content in Chapter 5, we see much more targeted metrics in the community/ambassador phase.

Are your employees tagged into relevant conversations, and not just conversations about the brand or its products, but relevant topics in the industry? For example, in Chapter 3 on elements of the playground, we looked at how the Atlassian Team Playbook includes multiple content depths and intents. It's clear that Atlassian is all about improving teamwork. When people discuss practices related to leadership, indicators of a healthy team, or different phases of building a team, that's relevant to Atlassian, regardless of whether someone buys an Atlassian product. Thus, Atlassian marketers are thrilled when they discover people talking about teamwork, particularly if they see that an Atlassian customer or employee is also engaging in the conversation.

The brand handle doesn't need to jump in and immediately share a link to the Team Playbook to add and receive value from the conversation. Others sharing a link, mentioning practices they learned by consuming Atlassian content, or tagging an Atlassian employee into the conversation are excellent indicators that the teamwork message is associated with Atlassian.

Clearly, this is much more difficult to track, since the brand might not be "officially" included in the conversation at all! (Typical metrics used along the social media spectrum are summarized in Figure 6.2.)

Figure 6.2   Metrics Across the Social Media Spectrum

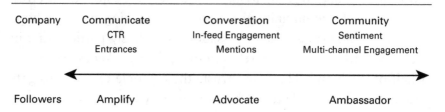

Company	Communicate	Conversation	Community
	CTR	In-feed Engagement	Sentiment
	Entrances	Mentions	Multi-channel Engagement
Followers	Amplify	Advocate	Ambassador

Improving the Communication and Amplification End of the Spectrum

We won't spend too much time focused on the communication and amplification end of the spectrum, but we do need to address this type of content and distribution. In some cases, brands and individuals do need to share information, and audiences do want to consume that information. The key is focusing on how best to meet this informational need for the audience.

The following are some examples of the mindset shifts:

- From "We're hosting a webinar" to "What will the audience learn if they attend this webinar?"
- From "We need to announce that we won an award" to "Why do our customers care about this award?"
- From "We're hiring; here's a job post" to "Why does a candidate want to apply for this role and work for our company?"

We can apply several of the principles we discussed about building the audience journey as a playground, including content depths and intent.

The key to communicating well is to lead with the benefits to the audience, not just the information, and help the audience understand why they should click to read or watch more, review the product or service, or join the event. What action should they take, based on the information you shared?

For example, instead of simply announcing the launch of a new product or feature, consider sharing a demo video of a key use case, or including customer quotes that show the value they received from beta-testing the new product. This represents tactical, buy-intent content that tells the audience exactly why they should buy. There's no generic, "We're excited for the launch of [feature]" copy, and no vague, "Check it out" CTA. The content shows the audience the value of the solution, right in the feed.

This isn't just for brand handles or company pages; it applies to employee posts as well. Companies often ask their employees to share the link to the latest product launch announcement, with pre-written copy about the high-level use case or general "excitement" sentiment, but this doesn't help the audience understand why they should care. Instead, employees should personalize the content for their audience.

For example, consider Goldcast, an AI-video editing and events hosting platform, primarily targeting B2B marketers as the core users. When it announced the availability of Goldcast Content Lab, its employees shared content about the launch on social media. One of the marketing team members included a 60-second video showcasing key features, such as editing out filler words, choosing key moments to trim from longer videos, and examples of different layouts for each distribution channel. The opening frame and thumbnail reads, "Amplify your B2B events," telling the viewer exactly what this tool helps you accomplish. The first 10 seconds of the video includes a summary of the tool, "Take your event content and create instant snackable clips."[2]

The post copy from the employee includes a clear value proposition: "No more waiting weeks to produce video content from your events! Say goodbye to spending hours trying to become a video editor on the spot." She goes on to share more details about key features that help you save time when creating additional content from event source material.

Meanwhile, one of the co-founders shared a different 60-second video to announce the waiting list for Goldcast Content Lab and focus more on extending authentic content. The video showcased the lifecycle of a specific interview, with participant names and more personalized pain-points.

Each person tailored the content to the needs of their audience. The marketer focused on a narrower set of pain-points around editing videos when video editing is not your core skill set, while the co-founder chose to extend moments of authentic connection by creating more personalized content. Both posts attracted positive comments and reactions, but from slightly different people within their target market. The marketer's post attracted in-house marketers in bigger companies, while the co-founder's post attracted more solopreneurs and leaders of lean marketing teams.

Regardless of whether the viewer watches the entire video, reads the entire post, or clicks the link to the Goldcast website, they will know which problem the product solves, along with some key features. Yes, the company gave information about the waiting list and general availability of the product, but it went beyond the usual thin copy to truly show the audience why they should watch the video, read the post, and ultimately, check out the product.

It's easy to think about buy-intent or use-intent content, since it has a distinct next action associated with it, but what about trust- or affinity-intent content? The "next action" is often just a feeling or change in perception. There's not much the audience should do after consuming this content. For example, many teams think that recognition posts are meant to build trust or affinity, so simply sharing that they won an award, brought in a new leader, or acquired a new customer is sufficient. But why should the audience care about this information, right now?

Consider pairing information like this with a timely event, instead of creating a stand-alone post. For example, awards about being the "best employer" or "great place to work" are not particularly dependent on the exact time of the award, but they are timely when the company is hiring. So, pairing the award information with a post about open roles makes it relevant for the audience. The post focuses on helping job seekers understand why they should apply to a role, instead of just informing the masses that the company won an award.

The same applies to the announcement of a new leader. Why does your audience care about this change? Does it affect how investors view the strength of the company? Will this person heavily influence the product roadmap or solution offerings for your customers? Focus on the benefits this person brings to your shareholders, stakeholders, and customers, instead of simply announcing the leadership change. This is also the perfect opportunity for the brand to present the new leader. The leader creates a post to share on their personal social media platforms, and the brand reacts, comments, or reshares their announcement. It gives the person an opportunity to showcase their excitement about the new opportunity, and it gives the brand a more human story as part of the announcement.

IMPROVE COMMUNICATION ON SOCIAL MEDIA

As you consider how best to communicate on social media, think about creative ways to bring your message to life. I've used the following ideas throughout my career:

- **Hiring:** Instead of simply posting the link to a role, create a carousel or story that tells candidates a bit about the company, team, role, and hiring manager. This is a great place to feature awards for "fastest growing start-up" or "best employer." Stand-alone posts about the awards feel shallow, but the external proof about the health and culture of the company helps candidates understand why they should apply.

- **Product or feature launches:** Ask your product managers to share the journey of building the new capabilities, including challenges, how they overcame these, and why they're proud to ship. This allows the marketing team to package up a few similar assets, such as videos or screenshots, without spamming the feeds with the same message. Then the product managers share their own excitement, in their own voice, in a way that resonates with their audience. The brand handle reuses this content to keep the momentum going, either by sharing the posts, or creating a round-up of the content for an original post from the brand handle.

- **Webinars, events, or office hours:** Offer a sneak-peek of the content! This works particularly well for content showcasing a new use case or solving a specific problem. The poster gives a preview of one or two features, with the CTA to join the event to see an additional couple of features in action. The goal is not to leave a cliff-hanger, but to provide enough value in the feed for the audience to see that joining the event provides even more value.

These types of broadcast content are most susceptible to algorithm suppression, in part because they rarely offer value directly in the feed. Yes, brands do need to share information sometimes, and that might include posting a URL for someone to learn more about the content. But, the algorithms change often, so work with an expert to make sure you're sharing according to the current best practices.

Conclusion

Social media is a place for humans to foster genuine relationships, built on a foundation of trust, with moments of delight. This means that brands must move beyond simply communicating information about themselves and asking their followers to amplify that information.

Of course, people do need information, but brands should focus on adding value for the audience when they communicate that information. Instead of forcing the audience to click on a link that takes them away from the current platform, brands should make the information available without the link. They must include benefits for the audience, and connect announcements about product launches, awards, and other company news directly to the needs of the consumer.

In the next two chapters, we'll look at tactics to move from the conversation end of the spectrum to focusing on engaging in conversations and fostering community.

Chapter Summary

- The social media spectrum consists of three pairings: communicate/amplify, conversation/advocacy, and community/ambassador. Brands need to move beyond simply communicating information and asking their followers to amplify that content.

- The metrics change depending on the position on the spectrum. Key metrics at the communicate/amplify end of the spectrum include click-through rate and entrances to owned properties. Key metrics in the conversation/advocacy phase include in-feed engagement and mentions. It is more difficult to measure the community/ambassador end of the spectrum, but key metrics here include sentiment and multi-channel engagement.

- To improve in the communicate/amplify phase, brands must understand and adhere to the best practices for sharing on each platform. They must show the benefits of the information to the audience, directly in the feed or on the native platform.

Notes

1 Natividad, A. (2022) Zero-Click Content: The Counterintuitive Way to Succeed in a Platform-Native World, SparkToro blog, July 25,

sparktoro.com/blog/zero-click-content-the-counterintuitive-way-to-succeed-in-a-platform-native-world (archived at https://perma.cc/B7UT-M3NQ)

2 McGuire, L. (2024) Content Lab is Officially Here!, LinkedIn post, March 11, linkedin.com/posts/lindsayladeroute_content-lab-is-officially-here-yea-it-activity-7123044561316184064-nj-I (archived at https://perma.cc/T5R6-U6NW)

Engage in Conversations on Social Media 07

Social media is no longer a place for brands to simply communicate with their audience. Instead, brands need to shift their mindset to strategies and tactics that focus on engaging in conversations with the audience, and building communities, both online and offline.

As we saw in Chapter 6, which introduced the social media spectrum, brands need to move from using social media solely as a distribution channel for company- and product-related content. Instead, they need to focus on building trust, relationships, and rapport with their audiences. Practically, this means creating audience-focused content, and engaging in multi-way conversations with people at all levels of seniority, notoriety, and likelihood of buying.

It may seem counterintuitive to engage with so many different audience members if your goal is to use social media to increase the likelihood of making a purchase, but we know it takes time to build trust, and many buyers are not currently in the market. And buyer profiles can change over time. Today's coordinator progresses to become tomorrow's decision-maker. Today's account champion might move to another company to become tomorrow's champion, but in an earlier stage of the buying cycle.

Social media is no longer simply a place to post links to the company website or product tour, so how do brands find, engage, and convert their audience with the new rules of social media?

Explore the New Rules of Social Media

In order to produce the right combination of communication, conversation, and community, marketers need to play by different rules. In this chapter, we'll discuss the following shifts:

- Non-scalable activities
- Prioritize in-feed engagement over CTR
- Prioritize audience preferences over brand guidelines
- Leverage emerging styles and platforms
- Establish a symbiotic relationship with employees
- Engage the whole human
- Partner with the ambassadors.

Non-Scalable Activities

Many companies want to prioritize scale, with the ability to reach as many people as possible, generate as many reactions, comments, followers, entrances, and clicks as possible, and hopefully, generate as much pipeline as possible. Particularly in SaaS businesses, the pressure to grow exponentially means that many marketers focus on activities that scale immediately. For example, paid media simply requires more dollars, rolling out features that are quick to build so that you can say you're always shipping, and looking for big names to attract an audience.

Sweet Fish Media, however, chose a different path. It performs activities that *don't* scale; not now, and not in the future. It's focused on building deep relationships and creating expert content that can't be replicated by the many AI tools entering the market.

Sweet Fish Media started as a podcast production company, but pivoted to help companies think like creators to build owned media capabilities. It builds credibility and trust with the target audience by creating deep relationships with experts in the space and curating niche content with those experts.

For example, Sweet Fish opened the Creator House in Orlando, Florida, and hosted its first roundtable in the fall of 2023. The Creator House is set up to make it easy to create content, with an intimate audio-only podcast space, newsroom-style set-up with multiple desk and backdrop options, a roundtable space for up to six speakers, and a casual couch for fireside chats. The spaces are left intact to make it easy to hop onto a mic for a quick podcast conversation or create a multi-camera, multi-angle video series. While the Creator House is optimized for content creation, it's also perfect for connection. There are four bedrooms, an upstairs living room, a full kitchen with plenty of seating, and a casual backyard with a patio, pool, and fire pit. The team advertises the Creator House for content creation and team off-sites, noting that you can have great conversations, no matter how or if they're captured.

Clearly, this is not scalable. It's unlikely that Sweet Fish will start buying up houses all over the world, staffing them with film and hospitality crew, and flying multiple creators out every quarter. The money and human resources required would make it difficult to turn a profit! Nonetheless, the Creator House is already making its mark. For example, James Carbary, the founder of Sweet Fish and the Creator House, uses his LinkedIn connections to bring together creators with an engaged following.

Many of these creators sit in the ideal customer profile for Sweet Fish. They're working in-house at companies with budget to hire an agency like Sweet Fish, they've bought in on the concept of brands thinking more like media companies, and they're progressive thinkers in the marketing space. This means that conversations recorded during roundtable sessions are insightful and, often, provocative. Further, the distribution is built in, since all the creators actively share and engage on social media platforms like LinkedIn.

Sweet Fish creates video clips of candid moments with participants and catchy soundbites from roundtable conversations. It shares these snippets on its company handles and employee handles, and gives all participants access to the clips to share via their own feeds. The reach is further extended, and credibility heightened, if the creators' brand handles engage in the content.

So, this tactic can't grow exponentially, and won't draw hundreds or thousands of people to the space in a single event, but the curated conversations with industry experts and high-touch, exclusive experience give the Creator House an outsized advantage when it comes to trust, content quality, and long-tail distribution.

This real-world example gives some practical guidelines for choosing which non-scalable activities are worth the time, effort, and money. First, think about what your audience can't get from anyone else. Is it an experience? A meeting with a specific person they'd love to talk to? A sneak-peek at an upcoming launch? Many teams think that simply spending lots of money on a nice meal or extravagant outing makes it "exclusive." But this means that competitors can simply copy the tactic by spending equal or more money to woo the same audience.

Second, think about how you'll use the exclusive nature of the offering throughout your marketing mix. You might choose to intentionally shroud it in mystery, taking no photos or videos, and only allowing the event, experience, or item to live on via word of mouth. Alternatively, you might equip participants with their own cameras and mics to help spread the message.

Last, think critically about how you'll measure success to determine the ROI of the activity. When you stop focusing on posting huge numbers, you need to find ways to put a value on the activity. "Building the relationship" might be the ultimate outcome, but what evidence do you have that you did strengthen the relationship through this engagement? In this case, you might look at softer signals, such as how many times the person posted about the experience on social media, referrals for other people in their network to join the next iteration of the engagement, and response rates the next time you reach out to them.

Prioritize In-Feed Engagement Over CTR

As we discussed in Chapter 5, marketers must go beyond click-through rate as the primary measure of success on social media. Platforms and audiences don't want to click to another platform to consume valuable content. This mindset shift dovetails with tactics like partnering with ambassadors and creating a symbiotic relationship with your employees.

For example, consider the traditional product or feature launch announcement on social media. Most companies write a short post on the company page, with a link to explore the product. It usually reads, "It's launch day! We're excited to share that [new feature] is now available in [product]. Read the blog to learn more about [benefits of new feature]." They include a link directly in the post, which generates a preview image that, if they've formatted it correctly, showcases a screenshot of the new feature. Then they furiously refresh the reporting dashboard to see how many people clicked the link from the post, reporting on the success of the social media efforts based on clicks and referral traffic. Unfortunately, many are disappointed to find that the announcement post doesn't drive a significant number of new entrances, let alone sign-ups or trials of the new feature. In contrast, I've worked with several teams to bring more humans into the launch strategy, which builds rapport and generates conversation about the offering.

Companies that sell products usually have product managers (PMs) on each team. These people help translate customer needs into product features, they create the overall roadmap for each release, and they work with the design and engineering teams to turn ideas into reality. When a new feature or product launches, they're thrilled. Unfortunately, most of that enthusiasm is locked in internal channels, like the quarterly business review, Slack announcement, or town hall slide.

Instead, brands can work with PMs to authentically share on their own social media profiles. This works particularly well on LinkedIn, where PMs can create carousels that showcase screenshots of the product. It's also helpful to include customer feedback from the journey and testimonials from early users of the new product or feature. This brings a more human tone to the announcement, and allows each PM to customize the information, based on their contribution to the new offering.

How would you measure this effort? You can look at impressions, reactions and comments on individual posts, and aggregate these metrics, in tandem with your company profile metrics, to understand reach and engagement. You might also look at the sentiment in the comments to understand how potential customers and users react to the news. In many cases, the personal announcement results in direct messages from the PM's network, which leads to deeper engagement with a potential customer.

I've personally seen the power of engaging publicly and continuing the conversation via direct messages. For example, a podcast host shared a link to their interview with executives from my company on LinkedIn. A commenter noted that they were vaguely familiar with one of our products, but they didn't realize it was made by the company featured in the episode. They asked for a marketer to reply with a bit more information. I skimmed their profile, noting their role and some of the challenges they talked about in their LinkedIn posts. I used this to inform which products and resources to share with them. I responded to their comment with a few links, mentioning that I'd be happy to share more if they needed anything else. The commenter sent me a direct message, thanking me for the thoughtful response. It turns out that they sat on the organizing committee for a conference that was heavily attended by one of our key personas, and they asked if I would be open to speaking at the conference. I introduced them to a colleague with more relevant background and expertise, and we were able to turn a random comment into a breakout session at the conference.

That interaction is not easily tracked, and CTR doesn't capture the true value of it. The value happened directly in the LinkedIn comments and direct messages via a personal profile and didn't enter the formal company channels until we moved into planning the breakout session logistics. Click-through rate is only one small indicator of the value exchange available on social media, and often underperforms compared to native interactions.

Prioritize Audience Preferences Over Brand Guidelines

Companies spend a lot of time and money defining their visual identity and brand guidelines, so they're often unwilling to stray from the rules.

Yet, platforms and audiences don't always reward content that follows brand guidelines.

For example, Instagram reels and TikTok gave rise to vertical video as a popular orientation. LinkedIn began rolling out a new tab dedicated to vertical video in summer 2024 after seeing the success of reels and TikTok videos. Many consumers watch videos on their phones, so the vertical format works particularly well for mobile viewing, but many brands remain reluctant to adopt this style of video, preferring the look of horizontal videos and the familiarity of creating this style of video content.

Many viewers watch videos without sound, so closed captions gained popularity. Closed captions are also good for accessibility, enabling viewers with certain disabilities to consume the content more easily. Unfortunately, many brands continue to expect their audience to watch videos with the sound up, and don't include captions or more visual storytelling.

With the rise of mobile videos, short-form video has also taken off, with viewers preferring to consume content in 30–60-second increments. Nonetheless, many brands continue to republish 30-minute breakout sessions, 60-minute webinars, and 90-minute keynotes!

Video is not the only form of content that has changed in the last few years. Visual content overall has changed as it has become easier for non-experts to create appealing content.

During the Covid-19 shutdowns, for example, marketing and social media teams could no longer rely on formal photoshoots or in-office opportunities to produce content for the company Instagram account. Instead, many turned to words on a flood of color to populate their feeds. This was particularly evident in brand campaigns for International Women's Day. Brands gathered quotes from female employees and ran multi-image carousels or a multi-day publishing cadence to highlight these quotes. Unfortunately, these posts fell flat, as the audience grew tired of seeing the same content over and over in their feeds. It was particularly evident for brands who featured a quote each day for a week. The first post received tens or hundreds of reactions, but the final post barely cracked double digits. The company account looked visually cohesive and on-brand, but it lacked personality and a human touch.

Instead of focusing on following traditional rules to create the best designs, or traditional means of creating video prior to mobile consumption, companies need to balance brand guidelines with user preferences. Allowing employees, influencers, and users to participate in the content creation process helps bring in authentic voices, and helps the company understand which types of content work best in each channel.

Highly curated content might make sense on Instagram but fail on LinkedIn. Spotlighting user-generated content (UGC) via Instagram Stories, for example, might be the perfect way to balance an on-brand account with frequent, authentic content.

Leverage Emerging Styles and Platforms

New social media platforms and trends enter the market frequently, and platforms tend to introduce similar features when they see the success of a feature on another platform. For example, Instagram introduced Threads, an app that is nearly identical to X. Many brands jumped on Threads when it went live because it gave them more ways to access their audience, and they could reuse most of the content they shared on X.

Similarly, many brands jump onto trend bandwagons, from showcasing the contents of the CEO's purse, to participating in challenges, pranks, or dances. For example, a meme gained popularity using a play on the phrase, "I'm a [role], of course I [action]," with different professionals sharing stereotypes of their role or industry. Another popular trend involved choreographed boxing between two individuals over a specific topic, where they pretended to throw punches to emphasize their point of view. These trends made the rounds on social media in early 2024, but faded quickly, as most social media trends do.

It means that brands need an opinion and a playbook about which trends they participate in, and which platforms to join as early adopters. If they don't move fast enough, they'll look like copycats, or miss the trend altogether. Or, if they jump on a meme too early or without context, they might alienate their audience. This is particularly true if the origin of the trend or meme has roots in groups that are histori-cally underrepresented, inside jokes with controversial origins, or completely false pretenses that result in the brand looking gullible.

This is even more tricky for platforms, since it takes time and consistent investment to grow by learning the rules of the audience, understanding the quirks of the algorithm, and building an engaged following. It's not simply acquiring the handle and occasionally post-ing the same content you have created for other channels. You need people to create the content according to the platform best practices, and you need people to monitor the account and engage with the audience. This means that it might not be the right decision to im-mediately jump on every new platform or feature that comes to market.

Consider Clubhouse, the viral audio app launched in early 2020.[1] Companies immediately jumped onto the new app, spinning up weekly rooms, chasing down high-profile guests to join their rooms, and hiring self-proclaimed experts to create and manage the new audio strategy. And yet, within a year, everyone asked, "Where's Clubhouse?" The spark caught and the app spread like wildfire, but the flame died out almost immediately. Companies were left with an underperforming channel, committed agency contracts, and in-house experts with little work to do.

Being an early adopter can bring significant rewards, and partici-pating in viral trends can help brands connect to larger audiences. But, understanding how each supports the overarching strategy and goals is essential for choosing the right moments and new platforms for investment.

Establish a Symbiotic Relationship with Employees

As we saw in Chapter 5, high-profile executives and founders fre-quently boast a larger social media following than the official brand handles, but executives and founders aren't the only ones with social media clout. Practitioners at all levels can build an audience, and, in some cases, may have more credibility with certain people than a senior-level executive.

Unfortunately, many brands try to create programs to force their employees to share company-related content. The programs are aptly named "employee amplification" or "employee advocacy" programs, indicating that the support flows in one direction: employees sharing, amplifying, engaging, and advocating for the company.

Brands should develop a symbiotic relationship with their employees. Instead of asking employees to engage on content shared from the brand handles, brand handles need to share, amplify, and engage with employee-generated content. And they should encourage and empower their employees to build personal brands on social media, create and share content on other sites like YouTube, and build their credibility and karma on forums like Reddit.

For example, consider Dreamdata, an attribution software company that went all-in on employee social media. After seeing the success of a few employees engaging on LinkedIn, it ran an all-company challenge to generate three million impressions on LinkedIn, purely through personal accounts. But the employees don't just promote the company's offerings.

Instead, the company hosts sessions to help employees learn more about best practices for sharing content on LinkedIn, exchange content ideas, and celebrate the wins each week. Employees are encouraged to share content on topics related to their core expertise. They're encouraged to share in a way they enjoy, including experimenting with memes and viral trends from other platforms, video, written, and static-image assets. And they're doing it all in public, talking about how they work with other employees to share more content, engage in comments, and reach their goals. The company page and leadership team boost the employee content by reacting and commenting. Peers engage with each other's content, creating a halo effect for each employee and the brand.

Naturally, other users are noticing! In fact, the Dreamdata team has been asked to host workshops and webinars about how to train teams on social selling tactics.

These initiatives drive real results for the Dreamdata team, with over 50 per cent of their sales accepted leads (SALs) attributed to social media, organic traffic, and direct searches, and many prospects telling the salesperson that they saw them on LinkedIn.[2]

Dreamdata also sold out its networking events at larger conferences, in large part due to the visibility of the team on LinkedIn. People know different members of the Dreamdata team, and follow them for help with selling, data and attribution, personal branding, and leadership. This means that when Dreamdata puts out an invitation for an event, attendees feel like they're meeting up with a friend rather than attending a brand activation.

While many Dreamdata employees have more followers than the company page, plenty of company pages have more followers than employee profiles. This means that when the brand handle engages with an employee's post, it increases the reach, due to the visibility of the brand. And these followers tend to be different from the employee's followers, which means that the engagement between a brand handle and an employee handle exposes each audience to the other.

Employees can also jump into more conversations in real time, giving a human face to the company and conversation. Many employees have built a network of their peers, which means that the conversation is relevant to their industry and skills. This is particularly valuable for large companies with extensive product or services portfolios, since it's difficult to have dedicated social media experts or leaders monitoring and engaging in every conversation, across multiple personas and topics.

Instead, let the peers who have trust within their network engage! They have credibility in the space because they work on these problems every day, and the activities are more scalable because colleagues are likely to already spend time in relevant online and offline spaces. Give guardrails about what employees can and can't share, but don't force them to copy and paste standard, generic answers.

If you see that a topic is gaining traction, work with the employee to create more robust content to address key questions and points of friction. This helps the company create timely content with genuine expertise, and it gives the employee more content to share in the conversation. It's a win for the company, a win for the employee, and a win for the audience.

LINKEDIN COMPANY PAGES AS A CHEERLEADER

Michelle J Raymond co-authored two books about using LinkedIn to increase business, and she's an expert on LinkedIn company pages. She helps companies and entrepreneurs improve their presence on LinkedIn, with a specific focus on the relationship between the branded company page and employees' profiles.

Michelle notes that brands need to shift their mindset about the company page on LinkedIn, treating it as a place to champion and cheer for employees, customers, and partners.[3] Many brands use their company page like a bulletin board, posting job requisitions, webinar announcements, and company news. They're static posts, meant to communicate basic information. And, similar to a physical bulletin board, few people interact with the content, and the information goes stale. It's hard to determine what value, if any, the posts provide.

Instead, the company page could be used to shine a spotlight on the humans behind the screen. Michelle suggests the following practical ways to turn the LinkedIn company page into a cheerleader:

- Recognize employee milestones and team achievements with a simple picture that captures the feeling of achievement, and add text that gives insight into the journey and the impact of the achievement. For example, when Michelle worked in manufacturing, the company celebrated the safety record, with longer and longer times since the last incident.

- Celebrate customer wins and invite conversations with users. Instead of sharing a link to a case study hosted on the company website, create a carousel of the benefits the customer experienced. Tag their company page and any individuals featured in the carousel, and invite them to join the conversation in the comments on the post.

- Share employee posts with comments about how the framework, strategies, or tactics make the company a great place to work or deliver outcomes for customers. Your employees are doing amazing things outside of the office, so showcase their non-profit work, or athletic or artistic endeavors. In the same way that you acknowledge your followers as whole humans, spotlight your employees as whole humans.

- Host "Ask Me Anything" sessions with company employees and leadership, and answer audience questions regularly.

This approach to company page content helps humanize the brand and encourages your audience to trust and engage with your humans behind the screen. It also builds the relationship with employees, and creates a positive feedback loop, as they feel recognized for their contributions and empowered to share those experiences on their own profiles.

Engage the Whole Human

We discussed the concept of "sonder" in the opening chapter on trust, which is the realization that everyone else is living a full, complex life, just like you. When we apply this to marketing, we realize that we need to treat our audience as whole humans, not just prospects, customers, or users.

On social media, this means we don't just treat people as followers that we can sell to. It's not just about followers consuming brand content or receiving engagement when we announce a milestone. Our followers have their own announcements, milestones, and heartaches. For companies who make the human connection a core part of their brand identity, they pay attention to moments that have little to do with the product or service the brand provides.

Consider Chewy, a consumer brand that sells pet food and supplies. It's well-known for excellent customer service and surprising moments that aim to delight their customers. For example, one gentleman recounted his experience with Chewy customer support. He called to see about a replacement for a defective item, and the customer service representative heard his newborn child crying in the background. She congratulated him on the new addition to the family and told him his replacement item was on the way. When he opened his Chewy package, the gentleman noticed a little something extra included in the box—a Chewy-branded onesie and the book *What Pet Should I Get?* by Dr. Seuss! The Chewy customer service representative had gone above and beyond to customize the package to acknowledge a big life milestone. The customer already appreciated her verbal acknowledgement over the phone, but this small inclusion of child-friendly items truly delighted him.

Chewy has many stories like this, from handwritten notes with a customer's first order, to sending flowers to owners whose pets have passed away. Chewy makes a point to acknowledge the whole human, at all stages of life. Even in moments that have little to do with their pets, Chewy knows that making the person feel valued is key to retaining customers, even with a higher price-point for their products.

You might think, "Well, it's easy for them, they have adorable animals on their side! What about those of us in a serious industry, with boring products?" And to that I say: There's still a human behind the screen.

Let's look at a different example that confirms this—an interaction between a customer of Atlassian and the company's social media team. Atlassian sells an incident communications product called Statuspage, which companies use to communicate the real-time status of a service to users. Its users are primarily IT professionals, support engineers, and customer support representatives, with a particular focus on more technical providers. Surely it's difficult for such a product to find ways to delight such an audience.

Yet, one day on X, the Atlassian social media team noticed something interesting—an account using Statuspage to report on a real-time "incident." This was no ordinary incident. In fact, this was a soon-to-be father, updating a personal instance of Statuspage about the birth of his first child. He titled the incident "Bebe Watch 2022" and posted updates about the progress of the impending birth. He used puns and word play that are common in his profession, quipping, "This might be the last time my wife and I have downtime for a while" and, "The doctors and nurses are optimistic about the arrival of our little engineer today!"

The Atlassian social team reached out to the poster directly to congratulate him on the new addition. They sent him a code for a gift from the "Lil Teammate" section of the Atlassian merchandise store to commemorate the resolution of the "incident."

Of course, the new dad was delighted, and soon posted the final update about the incident: His baby boy arrived, mom and baby were healthy, and he appreciated all the supportive comments on his Statuspage updates. As you can see, this user decided to bring a boring, technical product into one of his most intimate, life-changing moments. And the brand responded in kind, showing its human side by acknowledging this milestone.

Atlassian didn't sell more products that day. It didn't acquire a new user that day. And aside from the one public comment on the X thread, no one else saw the celebratory gesture. But for this user, the human connection was real and delightful. And it cost a few minutes of time and a small monetary token for the company to create this bonding moment.

So, as you think about delighting your customers and users, think beyond simply delighting them as customers and users! The focus on who people are in relation to your brand, your offering, and your revenue limits your ability to engage with them as real, whole humans. Yes, these people purchased your product or service to solve a problem, and, at minimum, your offering should perform as promised. But, when you think about what matters to the individuals in your audience outside of their day jobs, you build a much stronger relationship.

Partner With Ambassadors

As we have highlighted, people trust people like themselves. They seek out recommendations from their peers, and they ask people in their network for information before making a purchase. They also look for tips and tricks when using a product or tool and follow best practices to get the most out of services.

Some brands prefer to tightly control the narrative, content, and distribution of information, forcing prospects to fill out lengthy forms, or making it more difficult for customers to find and consume documentation. But savvy brands, meanwhile, realize the power of partnering with ambassadors. These people are brand fans, with lots of product knowledge and enthusiasm for talking about the brand, products, and services.

For example, consider George B. Thomas. He's an inbound marketer and HubSpot trainer with over 40 HubSpot certifications. His office is HubSpot orange, and he has a collection of INBOUND badges going back for years. His video backgrounds often feature HubSpot-related content, products, and event promotions. For those first discovering him, many assume George is a HubSpot employee. But he's not. He's a super fan!

Over the years, George has run multiple HubSpot learning and engagement spaces, including a podcast, *The Vault*, which features articles, videos, events, and more, and a hub called Sprocket Talk, with the tagline, "The Largest Unofficial HubSpot Resource." When you look at the content and branding, though, you'd be hard-pressed to separate Sprocket Talk from "official" HubSpot resources.

Some brands frown on this "unofficial" ambassadorship—but not HubSpot. It recognizes George as an outstanding partner in the quest to help marketers be better marketers. George builds genuine relationships, shares his expertise, and helps other marketers on their inbound journey. He is a regular speaker at the HubSpot INBOUND conference, and the company invited him to host the after-hours show when he's not speaking.

George has built a huge community of like-minded marketers, and evangelizes HubSpot as a tool, brand, and forward-thinker to his community. People like George resonate with their audiences precisely because they're *not* employees or formal brand spokespeople. They're passionate and knowledgeable, and they have the brand and their audience's best interests at heart. It makes them an excellent intermediary for brands because they're perceived as authentic.

These ambassadors are different from influencers (which we'll talk about in Chapter 11) because, generally, they're not paid, the company exerts little or no control over their content, and they go beyond focusing on promoting the brand and its offerings. True ambassadors "act as representatives and promoters of a specified activity." Notice that the definition does not say "of a specific company or party." Instead, these ambassadors have built credibility by talking about relevant topics, and discussing the tools and services that are useful within those topics.

For example, George goes beyond simply creating how-to videos about HubSpot products, and instead hosts conversations about a variety of marketing subjects, including trending topics such as AI in content marketing, YouTube marketing tactics, and merging older tactics with newer tactics. He also shares episodes on SMS marketing (short message service marketing), and how direct mail fits into an inbound marketing strategy.

When you're looking to partner with ambassadors, consider the following questions:

- What motivates this person?
- What are the risks to the brand if we elevate their voice?
- How might we support them to share broadly, accurately, and authentically?

The key is to approach these people as partners. Don't try to turn them into megaphones for the company or constantly try to police their content about the brand.

Conversation and Advocacy: Social Care in Action

As we saw in the definitions of each phase of the social media spectrum in Chapter 6, the widely used definition of "conversation" is an informal talk between two or more people, where they share news and exchange ideas. One key element that many brands miss is that a two-way conversation involves not only talking, but listening.

At the most basic level, companies monitor their feeds for at-mentions or people tagging the brand or product handles and branded hashtags. Most brands have started going beyond simply noting how many people are talking to them or about them by feeding these tags into a queue for employees to respond to. Many of the earlier examples in this chapter resulted from this type of monitoring, where brand handles and employees engaged with company-related content.

This approach resulted in two focus areas of responding to comments directly on branded posts, and handling customer support cases or customer complaints. With the advent of new technology, including chatbots and now AI, customers often turn to informal, immediate, text-based channels like social media over formal channels like submitting a case or making a phone call. And customers expect these channels to be "always on," particularly for large companies who serve a global audience. Their customers are logging on 24 hours a day, 7 days a week, from the Americas to Europe to India to Asia. This means that companies need to be available to respond in a timely manner, and they can no longer constrain customer service to a standard 9-to-5 schedule, Monday through Friday.

Going a step beyond basic monitoring and customer service, many social media teams have started implementing social listening tools to monitor conversations about relevant topics, company employees, and competitors. They use this information to uncover insights into common support issues, potential new competitors on the horizon, and possible brand advocates. The smartest teams send this information back into their customer research documents to inform the product or service roadmap, proactively create content that helps improve the customer experience, and understand new or deepening audience pain-points.

The Rise of Social Care

A comprehensive approach to conversation, which includes listening, responding, and taking additional actions as needed, is known as "social care," which goes beyond engagement management or social media moderation. Social care isn't just responding to inbound questions or negative sentiment, and it's not just deleting spammy comments or blocking trolls. Social care considers the entire conversation, throughout the audience, customer, and user journeys.

Fortunately, more and more teams say they're adopting or expanding their social care programs. According to *The State of Social Care Report* by B Squared Media, over 90 per cent of survey respondents in 2023 said they had a social care program. Over 50 per cent of respondents said they were "considering expanding" their social care program.[4]

Brooke Sellas, the founder and CEO of B Squared Media, helps clients expand their social media strategy to include comprehensive social care programs. She notes that dark mentions and tagging are key challenges for brands looking to be more proactive.[5] Dark mentions occur when a user talks about the brand or product lines without at-mentioning or tagging the company handle. In many cases, the users are trying to connect with other users rather than actively seeking a response from the brand. This means that, when a brand handle or company representative does chime in, they need to be mindful of their approach. It's not the time to respond with a generic message or sales-y approach. Instead, they should seek to understand, help, and ultimately, build trust.

B Squared Media helps clients consider different approaches to helping their customers and engaging on social media. For example, after reviewing the conversations about one client's premium coffee maker option, B Squared realized that users struggled to understand how to change the coffee filter. This information was clearly laid out in the manual, but it was too difficult to find, as evidenced by the widespread complaints and troubleshooting online. The company could have asked its social media team to respond to every mention with the page number from the manual. Instead, it recorded a short demo video, and shared it widely across its website, the product page, and social media. It addressed the immediate concern and improved the customer experience going forward.

Brooke notes that AI tools and capabilities can help companies tag, analyze, and improve their responses on social media. The AI insights help the humans on the team focus on the most impactful problems, conversations, and users, which helps them respond faster and provide answers to prevent future complaints.

As companies evolve beyond simple social media management or customer service via social media channels, they must also evolve their metrics. B Squared Media considers these core metrics to help answer the overarching question, "Can you easily name the top three reasons customers reached out on social media support over the last six months?" Metrics of how well these conversations are going include:

- **Response time:** The duration taken to respond to a customer's query or grievance

- **Resolution time:** The time required to fully address and rectify an acknowledged concern
- **Average first reply time:** The time elapsed before your team dispatches the initial reply to an inbound message during business hours
- **Average reply wait time:** Beyond the inaugural reply, this metric delineates the average waiting duration between subsequent responses
- **Total received messages:** A count of all inbound customer messages
- **Total replies or response volume:** The cumulative number of responses your team sends out
- **Reply or response rate:** The proportion of incoming messages that receive a reply
- **Resolution rate:** The percentage of customer inquiries that are fully addressed, shining light on inter-departmental collaboration efficacy
- **Most received topics and subtopics:** Key themes and topics frequenting your inbox, revealing audience interests and concerns
- **Positive and negative sentiment:** A metric capturing customer feelings and impressions about your brand
- **Voice of the customer data:** An invaluable metric that taps into genuine customer feedback, giving insights into behavior, preferences, pain points, and needs.

As you can see, a comprehensive approach to social care helps brands and their followers to continue deeper conversations.

Conclusion

The new rules of social media put humans at the center. Instead of focusing on company announcements or product launches, the new rules focus on the humans behind the screen, including employees, partners, customers, and industry experts.

The conversation phase of the social media spectrum helps companies move beyond distribution by incorporating listening, comments, and reacting to the content that their followers post.

To continue to build trust, rapport, and deep relationships with multiple audiences, brands need to continue to move to the community and ambassador end of the social media spectrum. In the next chapter, we'll discuss tactics to truly create community.

Chapter Summary

- The new rules of social media include non-scalable activities, prioritizing in-feed engagement over CTR and audience preferences over brand guidelines, leveraging emerging styles and platforms, creating a symbiotic relationship with employees, engaging the whole human, and partnering with ambassadors.

- In the conversation/advocacy phase of the social media spectrum, brands often assume they're driving conversations with and about the brand. Instead, they need to shift their mindset to listening to and engaging in relevant conversations with their followers.

- Social care is a comprehensive approach to listening, engaging, supporting, and improving the relationship between a company and its followers. It helps identify and resolve points of friction and find and provide moments of delight.

Notes

1 Davidson, P. and Seth, R. (2020) Check 1, 2, 3… Is This Thing On?, Clubhouse blog, July 11, blog.clubhouse.com/check-1-2-3 (archived at https://perma.cc/4T94-F478)

2 Erdem, L. (2024) Laura Erdem's Post, LinkedIn, February 1, linkedin. com/posts/lerdem_were-running-a-q1-challenge-for-a-revenue-activity-7155170991596331008-K0H6 (archived at https://perma.cc/76B7-2UJL)

3 Raymond, M.J. (2024) LinkedIn Page Advocacy: How to Turn Your Company Page into a Team Cheerleader! (podcast), B2B Growth Co,

August 7, socialmediaforb2bgrowthpodcast.com/episode/linkedin-page-advocacy-how-to-turn-your-company-page-into-a-team-cheerleader (archived at https://perma.cc/3WXS-CZVV)

4 Sellas, B. (2023) The State of Social Media Care, B Squared Media, bsquared.media/the-state-of-social-care-2023 (archived at https://perma.cc/4XLP-HL8J)

5 Sellas, B. (2024) The Rise of Social Care, interview with Ashley Faus, May 27.

The Power of Community: Online and Offline

08

The smartest and most successful brands go beyond communication and basic conversation. Instead, they focus on building communities, both online and offline. They take a holistic, decentralized approach to finding and connecting with multiple audience members.

Community-led growth has gained popularity as audiences become more skeptical of brands and desire instead to connect with individuals. People trust people like themselves, and they're seeking more intimate gatherings to find those people.

Of course, brands want to be in the middle of communities where their prospects and customers spend time. But, as individuals seek out communities that focus more on connecting individuals, they increasingly look to exclude brands from those spaces, with low tolerance for any whiff of pitching or advertising in their community spaces.

I framed this as a party in Chapter 6 when I introduced the community phase of the social media spectrum. If I invite a group of friends over to my house, it would be weird and awkward for me to stand up in the middle of the party, quieten the crowd, and start talking about myself. (I won an award! I'm looking for a new job. I tried a new cake recipe last week.) Then, after declaring these facts and milestones in the middle of the party, I expect all of my guests to applaud, stand in line to congratulate me or ask me questions, and eventually, help me polish my award plaque, introduce me to a hiring manager at their company, and join me in the kitchen next time I make a cake. This makes no sense, and my friends would be unlikely to accept an invitation to a party at my house in the future. Rightly so! They joined me because they wanted to relax, meet some other nice people, and enjoy the evening.

Unfortunately, many brands treat communities in the same wrong way. They join with the intention of pitching their offering or starting self-serving conversations instead of building genuine connections by participating as an equal. If we continue our party analogy, what role does a host play? They don't turn the evening into a monologue about themselves. Instead, they think about who to invite, ensuring that a nice mix of fun, interesting people join the party. They put out snacks and refill drinks throughout the evening. They move from group to group, joining conversations, making introductions, and ensuring everyone has a good time. In fact, some of the best parties result in guests meeting new people, who go on to become friends outside of the host's initial connection.

If brands want the benefits of building and engaging in community activities, they must shift their mindset away from short-term, self-seeking, transactional outcomes.

Dispelling Myths About Creating Communities

In the previous two chapters, we explored many tactics to improve conversation and advocacy, with a few examples of moving into the community and ambassador end of the social media spectrum. But, how can brands build and truly participate in communities with their users, fans, partners, and employees?

First, we need to dispel some common myths, starting with:

Myth: Brands own and lead the conversation.

Truth: Brands participate in and facilitate the conversation.

When brands engage with their users, fans, and employees, they organically build connections through the common experience of a challenge and interest in exploring solutions. This is why partnering with ambassadors like George B. Thomas (Chapter 6) and empowering employees to engage with their peers is so powerful. The brand contributes resources to help organize spaces for conversation, but the individuals bring credibility to build trust and relationships.

For example, consider how Help Scout engaged with an existing community called Support Driven. The community grew organically and was not associated with any brand. During her time as director of marketing at Help Scout, Devin Bramhall focused on aiding Help Scout employees, users, and customers to engage in the Support Driven community. Instead of inserting Help Scout initiatives into the existing event programming and other community spaces, she worked with the Support Driven founder, the Help Scout support team, and members of the existing community to provide financial support to enhance the established community experience.

Some of the tactics to support the Support Driven community included the following:

- Help Scout conducted and shared an annual salary study to help people in support roles understand and advocate for fair compensation in their roles.
- It offered giveaways like T-shirts and laptop stickers that celebrated support professionals, with the Help Scout brand taking a back seat. When teams attended Support Driven community events, they didn't need a sign: The community knew their faces and the brand because they participated as engaged members.
- Help Scout built a learning hub called HelpU, which provided education from both the company and the community. HelpU covered many different support-related topics, including people-first content, such as the Humans of Support series, and practical advice in the Help Desk Tips series.

Help Scout's participation in the large, engaged, existing community paid off. It was able to connect with industry influencers and people who were enthusiastic about the topic, which gave the company even more exposure to new audiences in its target market. It used high-value content created as part of its community efforts to convert visitors to its website into subscribers that it then nurtured. The take-away? Brands attract fans and customers when they participate in communities by adding value to the conversation.

The next myth to debunk is:

Myth: Only owned community counts.

Truth: Engage where your audience already spends time.

It can be attractive to some brands to build their own community because of the perceived benefits. It's a valuable asset, it's under the company's control, and it's much easier to measure impact when a brand owns a community platform. But, which is more valuable: control or efficacy?

Often, it is more effective and efficient to engage where your audience already spends time, instead of trying to force them into an owned property. Just like we need to provide value on native platforms, we also need to build community via native platforms.

Our final myth is:

Myth: Focus *only* on prospects and users.

Truth: Community includes all like-minded people.

As we've seen throughout these chapters, we need to shift the mindset away from community being "for" the brand and to make space "for" people to buy products. Instead, we should go back to the common definition of community as a feeling of connection in a group, based on shared goals, common interests, and similar attitudes and outlook. This means that a community includes enthusiasts, industry influencers, employees, partners, users, customers, and sometimes competitors.

Some companies create user groups that focus specifically on customers and users who want to learn best practices, hear about new features, and exchange tips with fellow customers, but these groups will not expand into larger community spaces if they continue to focus solely on existing customers. Instead, communities that expand take a more holistic view of the audience and their needs.

For example, the Cisco Developer Relations marketing team includes a dedicated community team and developer advocates. Their original purpose was to develop educational programming to support the people working with their products. Initially, they built a developer hub where employees and users actively engaged and helped each other figure out challenges. Over time, the community expanded to include non-users discussing industry challenges, not just product questions. Now, the space boasts thousands of posts and includes live meet-ups.

Cisco is not the only company with a strong community that grew out of an initial set of user groups. HubSpot also grew from HubSpot User Groups (aptly abbreviated to HUGs) into a thriving community of marketers, customer success professionals, salespeople, agencies and partners, and industry influencers. Similarly, Zapier offers spaces based on business interests or job family, including accounting and real estate. Its community includes core topics related to Zapier capabilities, discussions about why and when to automate certain workflows, and discussions about which creative tasks to automate, beyond common use cases.

As you think about building and engaging in communities, think beyond the sale. Users may be an excellent audience to start hosting, since they have an obvious connection to the brand and each other because they already use the product or service. However, if you want to grow a true community that builds trust and authentic connections, you need to make space for conversations that have nothing to do with buying or using the company's offerings.

Community and the Marketing Mix

Community strategy and tactics should exist throughout your marketing mix. Unfortunately, many companies approach community activities with a similar mindset to the linear funnel: it's a phase to be tacked on once someone becomes a customer. The foundation of this faulty assumption is the idea that customers are meant to become champions for the brand. If we convince them to buy, and they see value from the product, they'll tell their networks about our great offering. It's focused on a short-term buying outcome as the ultimate goal of engaging.

Figure 8.1   Community in the Linear Buyer's Journey

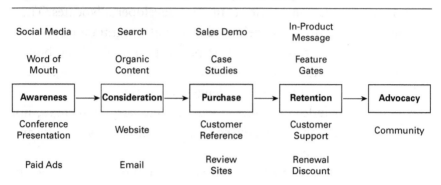

However, as we have seen in the mindset shift to the playground for other content spaces and audience journeys, community is not a final destination. It's an integrated, engaging part of the entire audience journey, regardless of whether or how quickly someone buys.

Let's reimagine the original linear journey with community as an end goal, moving from defined activities in each stage to a more holistic view of when and how community activities show up (Figure 8.1).

In reality, community elements should happen throughout the journey, and many of the channels, tasks, and assets throughout the journey have significant overlaps with community-related tactics.

For example, conferences, customer references, and customer support are all one-to-one ways in which employees and community ambassadors can engage with the audience via native platforms or owned community spaces. Conversations on social media help build awareness and affinity, and help unite third-party spaces with company-hosted spaces. Tactics such as providing custom swag and loyalty programs for long-term users dovetail with community efforts to build brand champions.

The following lists offer some ideas about how to incorporate community members into your other marketing activities.

Social media

- Host community groups on social platforms (LinkedIn groups, Reddit)

- Find influencers and enthusiasts already talking about your brand
- Engage in conversations to start a relationship
- Unite online and offline touchpoints
- Empower community members to be ambassadors on your behalf.

Events

- Host a Community Moderator dinner at an industry event or user conference
- Ask community members to share their experiences and takeaways for non-attendees
- Set up a roadshow-in-a-box and/or a train-the-trainer to extend content reach and engagement
- Invite active members to present sessions or join a panel.

Content marketing

- Offer bylines for trends and product use cases
- Amplify each other's content
- Showcase community-authored content in newsletters, ebooks, guides, and tutorials
- Invite community members to create demo videos.

Product marketing

- Invite them to be alpha and beta users
- Interview for customer research and feedback
- Solicit customer references
- Feature launch announcement sneak-peek and amplification
- Host Q&A sessions and Office Hours about the product.

As we'll see in Chapter 11 about working with subject-matter experts (SMEs) and influencers, many people want to build a personal brand and showcase their knowledge. In some cases, contributing to a knowledge base about a widely used product, speaking at a conference, and getting more involved with peer events can help to further a person's career.

Think about how you exchange value with your community members. It's not enough to host a space for them to converse, or occasionally provide food or fun T-shirts. Helping to position these members as experts with valuable skills and amplifying their voices to help them build a bigger personal platform adds value. Giving them early access to features and services, taking their feedback into consideration for the product roadmap, and connecting them with company leaders all add value.

Creating Community

Your community strategy should connect to your overall marketing strategy. As such, you'll need to conduct research to determine how best to engage.

Research

Start by creating a Venn diagram of the people you want to talk to and the relevant topics they're already discussing. The overlap represents the conversation sweet spot that acts as the foundation of the community. It's the "shared goals, common interests, and similar attitudes and outlook" portion of the definition of community.

KEY QUESTIONS TO ASK TO FIND THE CONVERSATION SWEET SPOT

People

- Who do you want to develop relationships with?
- Where do they engage with their community?
- Do your employees already engage in communities?

Topics

- What questions do your audience members ask?
- What shared interests do they discuss?
- What unique insights do you have to share?

Spaces

- Where are audiences already having conversations?
- Who else is active in these communities?
- What are the rules of engagement for brands?

You'll notice that many of these questions are similar to the questions we asked while designing our content strategy to fuel the playground journey, precisely because you should connect the community strategy to your other marketing activities. You can use the social media listening approach noted in Chapter 7 to glean insights about trending topics, where people spend time, and rules of engagement on different platforms.

Build Versus Join

Once you determine the conversation sweet spot, it's time to decide if you'll build your own community or join an existing community.

As you consider your approach, audit existing communities to determine where you might join the conversation, and which gaps you can fill. Note how many other community groups exist for your target audience and topics. What is the nature of those communities? Are they public, paid, semi-private, or hosted forums? Does it make sense to sponsor or partner with these organizations as a first step into the community space? Are there multiple similar communities that you could unify?

Once you spend time in the existing communities and forums, you'll start to see that members enforce unofficial or unspoken rules. You need to understand both if you want to succeed in those spaces, and watching how other communities evolve helps inform your own community culture if you decide to build something net-new.

Many companies default to trying to build their own community, complete with company logos and pre-populated topics, and requiring a password to engage. But, there are benefits to joining an existing company, as we saw with Help Scout's approach earlier in this chapter.

Let's compare the benefits of building a new, owned community versus joining an existing community.

Benefits of Building a Community

- Become the go-to space for that topic, particularly if you fill a gap in the market.
- Activities are easier to measure when you host a community space on an owned platform.
- You have more control over community culture and guidelines.
- The initial launch attracts attention for the brand.

Benefits of Joining a Community

- You can draft off existing momentum of a large membership and active forums.
- You can associate yourself with thought leaders and influencers.
- It is less expensive, with no start-up costs or ongoing resources for hosting and moderating.
- Employees might already engage in the community, which reduces friction for the brand entering the space.

Engage

Once you determine your approach to community, ongoing engagement is key. True community that builds relationships, affinity, and trust requires immersion and constant involvement.

In order to build continuity and depth, you need to show up consistently, in both content volume and cadence. Too many teams fail to make community a meaningful part of the marketing mix because they treat it like a campaign, with a flurry of activity for a month or two, and then silence as they evaluate the metrics before launching another flurry of assets. Community requires ongoing investment, so you need to ensure that you dedicate people to monitor, comment, and host.

The following are suggested guidelines on the approximate content mix to fuel your community engagement:

- Engage with community posts (70 per cent): A thriving community gives the microphone to the members, so focus on amplifying their voices by responding to threads and supporting their meet-ups.

- Employees and ambassadors post (30 per cent): These people seed discussions, share tips and tricks about the company's offerings, and answer support questions from users.

- Brand posts (Under 5 per cent): Similar to the overall social media strategy, sometimes members want to know information from the brand! Share announcements, request feedback, and host branded giveaways sparingly so that the community doesn't turn into an ongoing sales pitch.

Ensure that you bridge the online and offline touchpoints in your community strategy. The ability to meet in person helps build trust and rapport, which strengthens the online interactions as well. Community events don't need to be as formal and organized as a traditional conference or trade show, and brands should encourage members of the community to self-organize.

To support regional community connection, brands might fund food and beverages, offer space in a local office for the gathering, and dedicate resources to promote the event. Speakers should include a mix of employees, community members, and customers, and a community member should drive the agenda and format for most in-person gatherings.

Stand-alone communities often host regular, intimate gatherings, instead of one single large gathering. For example, Pavilion, a private, paid community for senior-level and C-level marketers, hosts multiple dinners each month in different cities. The groups are kept small, usually fewer than 20 attendees, to ensure that each attendee can interact with their peers on a deep level.

These offline gatherings are a perfect place to collect and create content for the online communities to extend the conversation and connections. Here are some practical ideas to bring offline community engagements to digital community spaces:

- Take a group picture at the dinner and share it on the community feed. This is an easy way to acknowledge the attendees and the energy during the event.

- Write a recap of some of the key questions and topics of discussion to continue the conversation and invite additional conversations with community members who couldn't attend the in-person gathering.

- Comment and react to attendees' posts on social media or owned community forums about the in-person gathering. It's not just about publicizing the brand or community owner's contribution; it's about continuing the discussion and supporting members' participation.

- Record videos with attendees about the in-person experience. This is an excellent way for brands and attendees to lean into trending memes or topics (for example, sharing what I'm wearing or what's in my purse).

Conclusion

Communities are a powerful way for brands to connect with individuals, including prospects, fans, potential and current employees, partners, advisors, industry experts and influencers, and even investors. When you gather a group of humans together, based on shared interests and experiences, you build trust and rapport that goes beyond a single transaction.

The key mindset shift required to create genuine community spaces and engagements? The brand is *not* the focus. The brand creates space for people to exchange ideas and perspectives and form their own peer groups with the brand as a facilitator. Communities offer powerful connections between companies and members, and help build trust and connection when approached with mutual respect and curiosity.

Chapter Summary

- Brands should approach community like a party host. A good host brings people together, helps everyone feel comfortable, and encourages participation in a fun and interesting experience.

- Communities are for all members, not just prospects or customers. Instead, community members should include employees, industry experts, influencers, partners, and fans, and go beyond focusing only on users or potential buyers of the brand's offering.

- Take a holistic approach to incorporating community activities into the marketing mix. Community spaces and community members should connect to your efforts across events, social media, content marketing, and product marketing. Community should not be a stand-alone program with siloed strategy and tactics. Instead, the activities should overlap, complement, and augment your overall marketing programs.

- Communities exist both online and offline. Make sure to connect your digital and in-person events, discussions, and participants.

Thought Leadership

09

Build and Maintain Trust Over Time

Thought leadership builds trust and influences buying decisions. Many companies make mistakes in their thought leadership programs, focusing too heavily on company- and product-related content to drive short-term sales. Instead, true thought leadership content changes minds and enables action in a new direction.

What is Thought Leadership?

Thought leadership is not a new topic. In fact, the term "thought leader" was coined by Joel Kurtzman, the editor-in-chief of *Strategy+business* magazine in 1994.[1] In the 30 years since the term entered the corporate lexicon, the definition has evolved, and strategies and tactics have changed. It remains quite vague, with blurred lines and continuing debates about who is a thought leader, what makes content "thought leadership," and how to use thought leaders and thought leadership content in the marketing mix.

Marketers, leaders, and consumers do agree that thought leadership is valuable. In their 2024 *Thought Leadership Impact Report*, Edelman and the LinkedIn B2B Institute found that 73 per cent of decision-makers surveyed said that thought leadership content is more trustworthy than marketing materials and product sheets.[2] We have seen, for example in Chapter 1 on trust, that people buy from people they trust. Thought leadership content helps consumers think differently about their business, challenges their understanding of the status quo, and acts as a catalyst for researching new problems and solutions.[3]

Decision-makers are more likely to buy from organizations that produce strong thought leadership content, and they're more likely to stay with a current provider that produces strong thought leadership content which confirms that the company continues to offer insights and solutions compared to competitors.[4]

In summary, thought leadership helps to build trust and adds value throughout the audience journey.

Unfortunately, the term "thought leadership" has a lot of baggage because too many people share a lot of fluff. They talk about a grand future where everything is amazing, but they don't share any plans for actually creating that future. They talk about how far they've come, triumphing over a big failure in the past, but they neglect to share any insights from their journey. They repeat quippy soundbites and hot takes, but they lack any nuance to help their audience improve.

Some people don't think it's important to define thought leadership, instead using the term to mean a variety of different things. From famous people, to contrarian ideas, to non-sales-y content, to marketers, executives and professionals in communications and PR, to self-proclaimed gurus, all use the term with multiple definitions.

I too wrestled with the definition of thought leadership, and struggled to come up with an answer as to why thought leadership is important, how to know if you are a thought leader, how to build thought leaders inside your organization, and how to measure the impact of thought leadership.

Over the next few chapters, we'll cover my four-pillar framework to help answer these questions. But first, we need to dispel some myths by talking about what thought leadership is not.

Thought Leadership is Not Quality Content

Leaders and practitioners often use "thought leadership" interchangeably with "quality content." They want to convey that we should put more effort into this particular asset. It should be better researched, share deep insights, and include more polished design elements. It should feel like a high-quality piece of content. In fact, *all* content should be quality content. Content across all intents, from buy-intent content such as a Product Tour webpage or Services Portfolio page, to help-intent content like product documentation or the agenda for Office Hours with your service provider, should meet the audience's needs in a delightful, seamless, and helpful way.

Thought Leadership is Not Executive Content

How often have you heard of teams calling any content that includes an executive or founder byline "thought leadership?" It happens all the time. But executives and founders frequently have bylines, appear in videos, and share content on stages—that isn't thought leadership.

Consider the quarterly earnings report. This is frequently delivered to investors and analysts by a chief executive officer (CEO), chief financial officer (CFO), or a founder. Yet, would you consider that content to be thought leadership? Probably not. Teams can easily understand that, just because an executive shares the information in an earnings report, it doesn't mean it's thought leadership, but they struggle to make this differentiation in other narratives and assets.

Thought Leadership is Not Why or How We Made Our Product or Service

Often, people think that talking about why you created something automatically makes it thought leadership content. As we saw when we discussed content depths in Chapter 3, the "why" is part of conceptual-depth content. But, as we also saw with many of the practical examples in that chapter, simply explaining why something is helpful or necessary does not make it thought leadership. Again, this is easy to understand with simple examples, like "why you should eat a high-protein diet (it's an essential ingredient for building big muscles)," but becomes much more difficult when translated to complex topics for brands.

Thought Leadership is Not Non-Product Content

Some teams think that sharing learn-intent content or assets related to stories and practices automatically means it's thought leadership content. This is incorrect. Learn-intent content often teaches the audience about existing information, including well-known topics, referencing older research. For example, we discussed in Chapter 4 how Atlassian shared articles related to Agile methodology on increasing reach, engagement, and conversion. While this learn-intent content is helpful, it's based on well-known practices that originated with other creators. Atlassian didn't create the concepts, despite articulating them in practical terms for teams looking to learn about incorporating Agile practices into their team rituals and workflows.

Thought Leadership is Not Being Contrarian

People often assume that being contrarian automatically makes you a thought leader, or that you must be contrarian if you want to be a thought leader. In theory, being at the forefront of your industry means that you're going against the best practices, status quo, and commonly held beliefs. You're introducing new ways of accomplishing something. You're iterating on previous work, which probably means you're dismantling some strategy and tactics, and that's going to ruffle some feathers!

Sharing in this way is different from being contrarian. Being contrarian for the sake of being contrarian doesn't make you a thought leader—it just makes you contrarian. Simply saying the opposite of whatever is trendy is not thought leadership. You must *add* to the conversation, not just change it.

Attributes of Thought Leadership

In the simplest terms, we can define thought leadership by looking at each word in the phrase. So, have thoughts, be a leader. If you look at the anatomy of the phrase, you see that "thought" is really about having something of value to say. Being a "leader" and showing "leadership" implies that you are worth following, and that people do, in fact, follow you.

True thought leadership content changes minds and enables action in a new direction. It balances lofty ideas with actionable insights.

Quality content is smart, helpful, and curated. It's not thought leadership, however, unless it's innovative, disruptive, and original. If we continue the three-word descriptions, we can say that a thought leader is someone who is smart, shaping, and sharing. Let's look at these attributes:

- **Smart**: You're an expert and you have actionable insights.
- **Sharing**: You codify your insights and make them available for others to learn, use, and improve.
- **Shaping**: You have influence in your industry, and your strategies and tactics become best practices.

Thought leadership is unique because it's about a differentiated point of view informed by expertise and experience, original ideas, strategy and/or execution, and helping the audience think, act, and achieve in new ways. Thought leadership builds trust because it's coming from someone with deep expertise and experience, and it enables someone to take action.

THOUGHT LEADERSHIP CONTENT
Edelman research

Edelman is a global communications firm with over 6,000 employees in 60 offices around the world. It helps organizations protect, promote, and improve their brand reputation.[5]

As part of its thought leadership content, Edelman conducts original research and longitudinal studies about topics related to its industry and ideal target persona. I've cited Edelman research several times throughout this book, including the Edelman Trust Barometer, and the *Thought Leadership Impact Report,* co-produced with LinkedIn.

As a communication and marketing firm, Edelman has the credibility to talk about building trust. In fact, it has established the Edelman Trust Institute to deep dive on this topic. The key, though, is that the company doesn't focus on itself. Instead, it has been conducting the survey on trust for two decades, sharing trends and insights about how others think, feel, and behave. It includes a large sample size from across the world, combined with insights from longitudinal analysis.

In 2018, Edelman started partnering with the LinkedIn B2B Institute to share insights about thought leadership and trust, citing some of its own research about the importance, foundations, and trends in trust.[6] The partnership expanded the content to include research and insights on timely topics and trends, including how different cultural and political lenses affect trust and reputation, the impact of artificial intelligence, and how new laws change the landscape for audiences. The publications go beyond simply sharing the theory or noting the facts found from the research, instead they translate these ideas and information into actionable insights and practical recommendations.

In addition to the written reports, Edelman expanded its content to include podcasts and virtual events, and built a strong following on multiple social media platforms, including over 570,000 followers on the company LinkedIn page, over 89,000 followers on X, and over 45,000 followers on Instagram. The research has been referenced by top publications including *The Wall Street Journal* and *The New York Times*, and has won many awards.

In sum, Edelman is an excellent example of a company that is smart, shaping, and sharing with the following activities:

- Original research related to its industry
- Ongoing analysis and insights, not one-off pieces of content
- Insights that are useful to others in adjacent industries, regardless of whether those people buy the Edelman product or service offering.

Pitfalls of Thought Leadership Programs

In addition to the misunderstanding of the meaning of thought leadership, many companies make mistakes when trying to build thought leaders and thought leadership programs, including the following.

Focusing Solely on Executives

Marketers and public relations professionals often shortlist executives to build as the organization's thought leaders. This is particularly true in founder-led companies, with the assumption that the founder is the best person to be a thought leader.

Unfortunately, executives often struggle to be thought leaders for several reasons. First, they're busy! These people often manage large organizations with tens or hundreds of people relying on them. They're responsible for a large budget, often owning the Profit & Loss statements, revenue goals and quotas, and customer growth numbers if they sit in the go-to-market organization, and efficiency, productivity, or cost savings if they sit on the engineering or IT side of the organization. This means that they don't have much time to experiment, iterate, and optimize, and then codify their findings in a way that others can follow. They don't have time to create quality assets. And they don't have time to distribute content in multiple channels, answer follow-up questions, or otherwise engage with the audience consistently to build a large following.

It turns out that practitioners throughout the organization are often better suited to growing into thought leaders because they're the ones grappling with the challenges and solving the complex problems. The audience trusts them because they bring real-world experience to the stories and solutions they share, and they're more likely to spend time on social media and build community with a larger peer network.

Second, the elements of being a thought leader and creating thought leadership content are often the exact opposite of what an executive does day in and day out. They spend a lot of time building consensus internally, reassuring employees and investors that the company is stable and growing, and carefully planning for short- and medium-term growth needs. This means that they worry about sharing an opinionated point of view externally, particularly one that's not fully tested, vetted, and repeatable at scale. What if it causes controversy and negative press coverage? What if it makes investors nervous about the direction of the company? What if it impacts the perception of customers and job candidates about the types of problems the company solves? These questions often work their way through legal, security, and communication team reviews. Unfortunately, by the time a new idea runs the gauntlet of vetting, executives are left with watered down PR or marketing speak, instead of an opinionated, differentiated, and actionable point of view. Leaders in the C-suite struggle to share these disruptive ideas because they've been told not to rock the boat in every other aspect of the business.

Outsourcing and Ghostwriting to Generate Thought Leadership Content

To mitigate concerns over the "busy executive" or the "SME who isn't a great content creator," many marketers focus on outsourcing elements of the thought leadership program and finding ghostwriters to create content on behalf of executives and subject-matter experts.

This mindset, however, assumes that it's just an execution problem. If we can just find someone to put pen to paper, we can produce a bunch of content. If we can find someone to pitch to conferences and industry publications, we can distribute the thought leadership. If we can just get a designer and editor, we can turn one asset into several assets to fuel a campaign. If we can just get someone to schedule everything, we can fill the calendar. With the advent of AI, we can just ask the robots to write and share everything!

But you can't outsource thinking. As we have just seen, thought leadership requires the person to share a differentiated point of view, informed by expertise and experience, including original ideas and actionable insights. The person who's meant to be a thought leader needs to actually have thoughts!

Yes, someone can help you pitch.

Yes, someone can help you schedule.

Yes, someone can help you repurpose.

But, at some point, original thinking must be done.

That thinking doesn't have to be done in public, or be fully finished, or perfectly stated. In fact, the thinking is often messy—and that's a good thing, because exploration to find something novel takes time and failure and detours. If your team wants to create and distribute thought leadership content, you need a thought leader who is willing to take the time to codify their ideas into something shareable.

This is why ghostwriting is not a solution, because ghostwriting can't be done if you don't have a large body of existing work to understand the person's unique voice and tone, if you're missing a large body of existing ideas, arguments, and examples, and you don't have a credible person to attribute the byline to.

Yes, writers can produce a lot of content, and that content can be quite smart, but if they're doing all the research, all the writing, all the publishing, and all the distribution, they're not ghostwriting—they're acting as the SME, bordering on being the thought leader.

Ghostwriting implies that you're "being a ghost" of someone. It means that someone must exist and collaborate, so the ghostwriter simply reshapes the ideas and words they already share. Unfortunately, many teams want a ghost-thinker. Far too often, "just get someone to ghostwrite it" is an excuse to let busy people off the hook of doing the hard work of identifying, packaging, and distributing smart ideas into smart content. For ghostwriting to be truly effective, teams and leaders need to dedicate the time, focus, and energy to giving the ghostwriter something to actually "ghost."

In sum, no number of brilliant writers, capable communications folks, or administrative professionals who can wrangle a calendar will help if you don't have a leader with thoughts.

Business Activities Versus Thought Leadership Activities

Every team needs to make trade-offs, and people often ask, "Should we prioritize business activities or thought leadership activities?" But this is a false dichotomy. Thought leadership activities *are* business activities.

Teams get it wrong when they turn thought leadership into short-term sales content (the mistake mentioned at the beginning of this section, about focusing on why the company built the product or service). They also get it wrong when they disconnect thought leadership from the rest of the business.

Thought leadership requires you to have credibility and strong depth of ideas. This means that you need to be an SME in your topic area, you need to be connected to your audience, and you need to understand and acknowledge current trends. You can't add to, change, or influence the future of the conversation or how your audience thinks about the topic and acts on the ideas if you're completely disconnected from the current state. Nor will you have credibility to share your novel ideas as a brand if they aren't connected in some way to the areas you're already known for.

Marketers have seen this go wrong with tactics like greenwashing or trend-jacking, where the hook for thought leadership seems like it's coming out of nowhere. It's an attempt to somehow fool the audience, but they usually see right through it.

So, marketers need to reframe the mindset. Thought leadership activities are business activities.

The Four Pillars of Thought Leadership

Now that we have an overview of what thought leadership is and is not, we must figure out how to actually become a thought leader. I get this question all the time, "Are thought leaders born or made?" My resounding answer is, "Thought leaders are made!"

I say this based on the four-pillar framework I developed to answer the following questions: How do you know if you're a thought leader? How do you measure progress towards becoming a thought leader? Are there strategies and tactics to accelerate thought leadership?

The four pillars of thought leadership, which will be discussed in detail in Chapter 10, are:

- Credibility
- Profile
- Prolific
- Strong depth of ideas.

Before we dive into each pillar, we need to put some guardrails in place. These guardrails tend to work well for B2B companies, and they work particularly well for the conversations I've had in my current and previous companies. Understanding that you operate in a specific area of knowledge and a defined sphere of influence guides how you implement the tactics in each pillar.

- **The framework focuses on knowledge workers, not celebrities.** If you just want to be "famous," there's a lot of not-aligned-to-business-goals ways to get there. In fact, some sort of scandal is actually an excellent way to put your company or employees on the map! But I assume that's not what you want when you seek advice on thought leadership.

- **You need to have a thought.** You need to be making improvements, executing in new or novel ways, or otherwise iterating and introducing something new or original. Simply delivering factual information about company performance, product launches or new services offerings, or documenting existing processes, does not make you a thought leader.

- **Being good at your job does not make you a thought leader.** Many employees and companies think that if someone is good at their job, they are a thought leader. Not necessarily. Building an external following is a requirement. Sharing externally is a requirement. If someone has no desire to take their knowledge outside of their team or make a bigger impact than their company or salary, they don't want to be a thought leader—and that's fine!

In the next chapter, we'll look the proof-points of each pillar, as well as tactics to help you grow across credibility, profile, prolific, and depth of ideas.

Conclusion

As you can see, defining and creating true thought leadership content and building thought leaders in your organization generates significant business value. People buy from people they trust, and thought leadership is essential to building trust with your audience.

It's not enough to simply create quality content. Companies need to shape the conversation by sharing smart content that helps their audience think in a new way and take action in a new direction.

Chapter Summary

- Thought leadership helps build trust and add value throughout the audience journey.
- Thought leadership content includes three key attributes: smart, shaping, and sharing.
- Avoid common pitfalls of thought leadership programs, including focusing solely on executives, outsourcing, and ghostwriting to generate thought leadership content, and creating a false dichotomy between business activities and thought leadership activities.

Notes

1 Kleiner, A. (2016) Remembering Joel Kurtzman, *Strategy+business*, April 10, www.strategy-business.com/blog/Remembering-Joel-Kurtzman (archived at https://perma.cc/C55B-N7NZ)

2 Kingsbury, J., Barik, T., et al. (2023) Reaching Beyond the Ready: Thought Leadership's Impact on Out-of-Market B2B Buyers, *2024 B2B Thought Leadership Impact Report*, edelman.com/expertise/Business-Marketing/2024-b2b-thought-leadership-report (archived at https://perma.cc/7JZW-XPK7)

3 Kingsbury, J., Barik, T., etc al. (2023)

4 Kingsbury, J., Barik, T., etc al. (2023)

5 Edelman (2024) About Edelman, edelman.com/about-us (archived at https://perma.cc/U89K-79PJ)

6 Kingsbury, J., Barik, T., etc al. (2023)

Four Pillars of Thought Leadership

10

Credibility, Profile, Prolific, Depth of Ideas

Thought leadership builds trust with your audience, but many marketing teams struggle to identify potential thought leaders in the organization, or grow these people consistently, and measure their progress and impact. Using the four pillars of thought leadership, teams can assess their current efforts, create a consistent and holistic plan, and build a pipeline to scale their thought leadership efforts.

As we saw in the previous chapter, thought leadership is a powerful way to build trust and authority with your audience, and helps decision-makers choose and remain with a solution provider. So, how do we build thought leaders in order to reap the benefits of creating and distributing thought leadership content? We'll use four pillars to understand proof-points and tactics to build thought leaders, which are:

- credibility
- profile
- prolific
- depth of ideas

The pillars work together in tandem, and true thought leaders are strong in all four pillars. There's no pillar that is more important, you must have all four (See Figure 10.1).

Figure 10.1 The Four Pillars of Thought Leadership

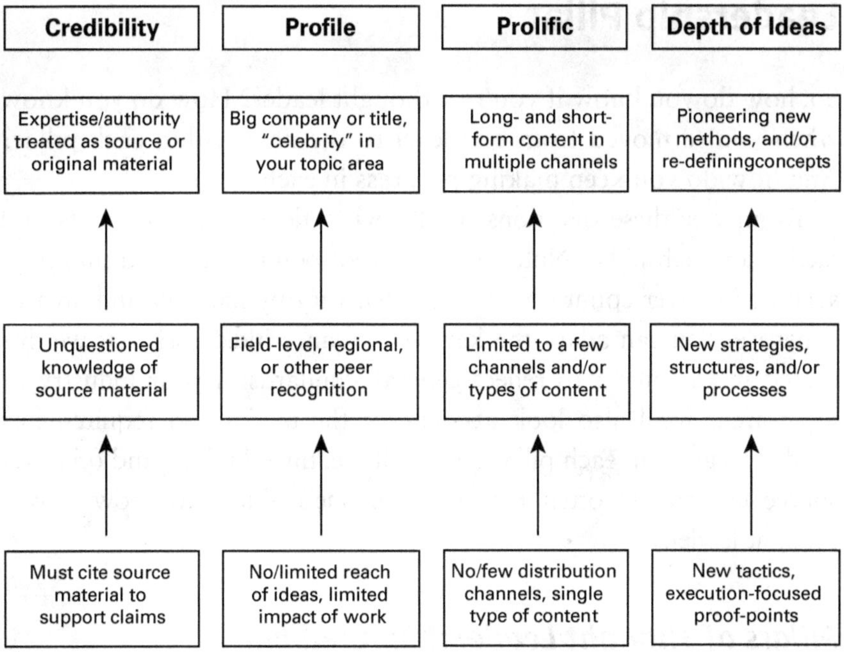

Credibility	Profile	Prolific	Depth of Ideas
Expertise/authority treated as source or original material	Big company or title, "celebrity" in your topic area	Long- and short-form content in multiple channels	Pioneering new methods, and/or re-definingconcepts
↑	↑	↑	↑
Unquestioned knowledge of source material	Field-level, regional, or other peer recognition	Limited to a few channels and/or types of content	New strategies, structures, and/or processes
↑	↑	↑	↑
Must cite source material to support claims	No/limited reach of ideas, limited impact of work	No/few distribution channels, single type of content	New tactics, execution-focused proof-points

Credibility is about whether people perceive you as an authority in your subject.

Profile is about how many people know you, and the nature of your connections.

Being prolific is about how often you share your knowledge, and the prestige of the outlets where you speak or publish. This is closely tied to having a strong profile because, as your profile improves, so do your opportunities to share with bigger audiences.

Depth of ideas is about codifying your insights into processes and frameworks that teach others how to replicate your success. Remember, it's not just about being good at your job, it's about codifying your expertise so that other people can learn, implement, and see success.

Proof-points and Tactics for Each Thought Leadership Pillar

So, how do you know if you're a thought leader? How do you know when you've moved from one level to the next within each pillar? And how do you keep making progress in each pillar?

To answer these questions, we'll review detailed proof-points and tactics for each pillar. Note that the proof-points with hard numbers, such as follower count on social media, vary by industry and area of expertise. You can adapt the key performance indicators that we discussed in Chapter 5 to reflect general standards in your industry or topic area. We'll also look at some of the tactics and requirements needed to grow in each pillar. As you'll see, time, budget, and other resource constraints often hamper someone's ability to grow into a thought leader.

Pillars of Thought Leadership: Credibility

Credibility is about whether you're viewed as an authority or subject-matter expert in your topic area. As you think about the credibility pillar, you must think about how the audience views you.

THE FOUR PILLARS OF THOUGHT LEADERSHIP: CREDIBILITY

Low level: Must cite source material to support claims.

Proof-points:

- Links to source material, requests for details to prove claims.
- Person may or may not be quoted, citations and links are always included to confirm credibility of the source.

Middle: Unquestioned knowledge of source material.

Proof-points:

- Says, "Study shows" or "Best practice is" and it's assumed to be true.

- Trusted outlets and experts quote them in conjunction with other citations or links.

High: Expertise/authority treated as source/original material.

Proof-points:

- Says, "X is true" or "I've done Y" and it's taken as a fact.
- Trusted outlets and experts quote them without additional supporting citations or links.

Tactics:

- Build one or more types of authority:
  o Positional (big title)
  o Credentials (education, certification, license)
  o SME or practitioner with repeatable results (years of experience, number of people helped).
- Regularly share a perspective on developments and research in the space that we're targeting.
- Fund research projects or testing strategies/tactics.
- Spend at least 20 per cent of time to conduct research and tests and codify ideas, methods, and results (note that these do not need to meet the level of a traditional peer-reviewed scientific study).
- Act as the spokesperson on behalf of the company, utilize the company's credibility as a halo (tell the company's story, share a scripted narrative).
- Partner with credible third-party individuals, publications, and brands to lend credibility to this person's ideas.

Do people believe what you say? Do people think you're knowledgeable? Do people trust you? As you grow in the credibility pillar, you'll see a shift from how often people ask you to cite your sources towards citing you as the source.

For example, in the early stages of the thought leadership journey, you'll need to provide multiple studies or quotes from other experts to prove your claims. In the middle of the journey, you can more generally state that studies show an outcome or frame your recommendations as best practices. At the mature phase of the journey, it's more likely that you can simply state something as fact, and other trustworthy sources of information will quote you as the source, without asking for additional citations.

Credibility can be positional, such as a title, a practitioner with repeatable results or extensive experience in the field, or through formal credentials like education and licenses. You can accelerate growth in the credibility pillar by pairing with a strong brand or another prominent thought leader in your field, and acting as a spokesperson on behalf of the company, even if you're not sharing new research, ideas, or insights.

To grow in this pillar, individuals need to do research, experiment and iterate, and measure the results of their experiments. They need time to actually test and implement their new or novel ideas, and they also need time to codify their findings.

It's not just about the individual who is trying to grow in the credibility pillar. They need willing and capable teams to test the frameworks and findings to help them confirm that the ideas work and give them input to continue building on their ideas, strategies, and tactics. Without a reasonable sample size, the person might have credibility, but the idea or actions might not.

Pillars of Thought Leadership: Profile

Growing a large following or being "famous" in your field is an important part of being a thought leader (Remember: Have thoughts, be a leader). You've heard people joke that only their mom or their spouse sees their content? They're signaling that they know they're not well-known and they don't get attention from high-reach outlets, individuals, or conferences. They don't have a profile.

THE FOUR PILLARS OF THOUGHT LEADERSHIP: PROFILE

Low level: No/limited reach of ideas, limited impact of work.
Proof-points:

- Limited sharing/traffic/attendance of talks, posts, and/or editorial content

- Pitch acceptance is tenuous for written and/or verbal outlets
- Personally known connections, fewer than 1,000 followers on social platforms.

Middle: Field-level, regional, or other peer recognition.

Proof-points:

- Shared/quoted by industry experts
- Pitches regularly accepted at industry conferences and niche publications
- 50/50 people who know you versus people you know, fewer than 5,000 followers on social platforms.

High: Big company or title, "celebrity" in your topic area.

Proof-points:

- Shared by trusted outlets and influencers
- Inbound requests from trusted outlets and influencers
- 90/10 people who know you versus people you know, more than 5,000 followers on social platforms.

Tactics:

- Share in owned personal and company channels:
  - Editorial content (personal and/or company blog, LinkedIn articles, and so on)
  - At least one social profile (priority given to LinkedIn).
- Republish on adjacent channels where you have strong influence or ownership.
- Share content that mentions you from outlets and people at or above your level.
- Follow influencers, brands, and publications, share their content regularly, and connect strategically with key influencers.
- Pitch appropriate tier (1, 2, or 3) conferences and outlets for your level:
  - Tier 1 and below at highest profile
  - Tier 2 and below at mid-level profile
  - Tier 3 and below at lowest profile.
- Accept inbound requests for content exchanges and speaking engagements.

One of the less obvious changes as you move up in this pillar is the nature of your network. People who are just starting out on building a profile personally know most of the connections they have, either through past workplaces, attending college together, or meeting at an event. But, as you move up, you start to see the opposite: connections know you, but you don't know them.

Other markers that you're well-known in your field include prestigious outlets featuring you rather than you sharing links to those outlets. Conferences invite you to speak rather than you pitching to speak. You're tagged into discussions on social media as someone who can answer questions, weigh in on debates, and share the latest trends. As your profile grows, you see that the prestige of the conferences, press or industry publications, and peers increases. Attempting to start at the top of the pyramid is a common pitfall in this pillar. It's unlikely that you'll secure the keynote at the largest industry conference or bylines in top-tier publications right at the beginning.

Instead, focus on pitching and accepting engagements with people and outlets of a similar-size profile. For example, you might start on a panel at a regional industry conference, work your way up to a breakout session at a regional or national conference, and, eventually, seek to present the keynote. Similarly, joining as a guest on a top-ranked podcast might be your goal at the top of the profile pillar, but you can start as a guest on smaller or niche podcasts. Don't turn down requests simply because an outlet is smaller or less well-known. These are opportunities to build your profile, expand your audience, and hone your ideas. It gives you proof-points when you're working to secure more prestigious engagements, to show that you have something interesting to say and you can say it well. It's also a way to network with new people, receive introductions to other conference organizers, podcast hosts, or industry publications, and connect with other leaders in your topic area or industry.

Growing in this pillar also means that you grow the size of your audience, both online and in person. The specific numbers vary by industry, topic area, and platform, so consider the total market for your ideas and which channels your audience frequents when you think about the number of followers required to move up in this pillar. You can look at other "big names" in the field for a reference.

When I initially created this framework, I stated that people with a low profile have fewer than 1,000 followers on the most important social media platform in their industry, around 5,000 followers in the middle of their journey, and significantly over 5,000 followers in the mature phase of the journey. However, these numbers are much higher in many cases. For example, Ann Handley, a best-selling author and chief content officer at MarketingProfs, has (early 2025) nearly 500,000 followers on LinkedIn and nearly 50,000 on X. Seth Godin, a household name in marketing, author, and founder of the altMBA, has over 250,000 followers on LinkedIn, and nearly 800,000 followers on X. Thus, a few thousand followers on either of these platforms is unlikely to mean you have a strong profile in the marketing industry.

Note that a large following on social media is not the only way to grow in the profile pillar. Consider Cal Newport, author of best-selling books *Deep Work*, *A World Without Email*, and *Digital Minimalism*. He barely shows up for searches on LinkedIn and X, yet he's written nine books and sold over two million copies of them. He has appeared on mass-media TV programs including *Good Morning America* and *The Today Show*, and he's featured on well-known podcasts, including NPR. Newport is a regular contributor to recognizable magazines such as *The New Yorker* and *Wired*, and has featured in mainstream media outlets including *The New York Times* and *The Wall Street Journal*.[1] Clearly, Newport has a strong profile, despite having a small following on social media, in large part because he's so prolific in other areas.

Pillars of Thought Leadership: Prolific

The prolific pillar is about creating and sharing your ideas widely and consistently. It's also the only pillar that is 100 per cent in your control as an individual. The other pillars are about how others perceive you and your ideas, but being prolific is about the actions you take.

THE FOUR PILLARS OF THOUGHT LEADERSHIP: PROLIFIC

Low level: No/few distribution channels, single type of content.

Proof-points:

- Owned channels (company or personal blog, personal social media handles)
- Single/limited content type(s) within your control
- Release fewer than six pieces of content per year.

Middle: Limited to a few channels and/or types of content.

Proof-points:

- Articles and quotes in niche outlets
- Breakout sessions and panels at industry conferences
- Variety of channel types (owned and earned across social, editorial, press, and speaking)
- Release fewer than 12 pieces of content per year.

High: Long- and short-form content in multiple channels.

Proof-points:

- Articles and quotes in mass media
- Keynotes at industry conferences and/or sessions at broad-reaching conferences
- Content spanning all types of assets and channels
- Release two or three pieces of content per month.

Tactics:

- Write for channels appropriate to your level. Reduce frequency of contributions to owned channels as profile and credibility increases in favor of trusted or far-reaching outlets.
- Pitch and accept speaking engagements appropriate to your level:
  - Low: Meet-ups, internal town halls, niche conferences
  - Mid: Strategic meet-ups, joint panels with other peers and experts, strategic educational institutions, industry conferences; accept as many local or virtual inbound requests as possible

- o High: Accept strategic inbound requests, pitch tier 1 conferences/podcasts, joint panels with other mid-high-profile experts only.
- Share on social media and engage with followers regularly.
- Pitch/offer quotes to outlets/influencers as appropriate to your level (high-profile individuals shouldn't give a quote to a random blogger with under 100 followers on social media).

Prolific people write blogs, speak at conferences, create videos, join podcasts, post on social media, and engage with their audience. They produce and share a lot of content.

Sometimes people think being prolific means creating net-new content all day, every day, on every channel. Instead, repurposing, reframing, and reorganizing are the keys to success. Yes, you need to share different types of content in different places regularly to build your credibility and profile, and help people learn from your depth of ideas, but remixing existing content saves time and allows you to share your message with new and different audiences. Prolific people use the tactics we discussed in Chapter 4 to create modular content and use a blend of decomposition and building blocks to create multiple asset types and populate multiple channels.

Being prolific is also about having lots of ideas and helping to hone the ideas that are most worth sharing. If you simply do the same work over and over or just repeat the same processes, you're unlikely to come across anything new and innovative. By writing, experimenting, and sharing, and debating the current trends, you're more likely to receive feedback and additional inputs to help you generate more and better ideas. This in turn leads to more discussion and adoption. It's a virtuous cycle of creativity, output, and audience building.

Many platforms reward consistent publishing and engagement. For example, the best practices for sharing on X are to post several times each day. On LinkedIn it's several times each week, and YouTube channels often have weekly or monthly video series. Most of these platforms also reward engaging with your followers, including commenting, reacting, or sharing others' content.

At the start of growing in this pillar, someone may only share once a month or every other month. As they grow, we expect to see them releasing content at least once per month. At the highest levels, thought leaders share two or three pieces of content per month.

As noted earlier, "content" does not necessarily mean a long-form article with thousands of words or an hour-long conference presentation. It can mean a LinkedIn carousel, a series of shorter posts on a community or industry forum, or snippets from a webinar or presentation. The goal is to share ideas and engage with the audience regularly. People can't adopt ideas that they don't know about or don't understand, so breaking down the concepts in multiple assets, channels, and angles helps you reach more people and enables your ideas to spread.

It's also important to set reasonable expectations about where to start sharing and engaging. As we saw in the profile pillar, you must match your expertise to the outlet. The same is true for being prolific. Start by sharing on your owned channels or your company channels. Don't let your content languish in the drafts folder simply because it hasn't been picked up by a prestigious outlet or accepted to a large conference. Give yourself deadlines to publish the content on your owned channels if the pitch is not accepted elsewhere, and, when possible, ask for permission to publish the content on other channels when you publish externally.

For example, many press and industry publications want exclusive, first-run articles, but they'll allow the author to republish the article on the company blog or the author's channels after a few weeks. You can include a backlink to the original article, and share both assets on your social media channels or linked from your website. For example, when I published content about rookie mistakes to avoid with the career site The Muse, I republished the piece as a LinkedIn article from my personal profile and included a note that it was originally published on The Muse, along with a backlink to the original piece.

Pillars of Thought Leadership: Depth of Ideas

The depth of ideas pillar makes up the "have thoughts" portion of the thought leadership phrase. It's about innovative ideas, strategies, and tactics, and sharing an opinionated and differentiated perspective that helps your audience take action in a new way.

THE FOUR PILLARS OF THOUGHT LEADERSHIP: DEPTH OF IDEAS

Low level: New tactics, execution-focused proof-points.

Proof-points:

- Codifying execution or tactics using tried-and-true strategies
- Tactics using data or research from your own field
- Team- or functional-level impact.

Middle: New strategies, structures, and/or processes.

Proof-points:

- Innovating on someone else's concept or methodology
- Using data and/or research from adjacent fields to improve in your own field
- Company-level impact.

High: Pioneering new methods, and/or redefining concepts.

Proof-points:

- Publishing in academic-adjacent journals and tier 1 media
- Statistically significant research and/or surveys
- Case studies about your approach and/or ideas
- Impact that is industry-level and beyond.

Tactics:

- Research time and budget appropriate to your level:
  - Low: Run experiments on owned projects with new tactics, documenting the results as a case study or tutorial.
  - Mid: Run experiments with internal teams or company-wide using new tactics, strategies, or processes and documenting results as a case study or tutorial.
  - High: Allocate time and money for others to use, test, and document their experience.

- Address problems appropriate to your level:
  - o Low: Tackle problems in the organization that other brands, organizations, or influencers have solved before.
  - o Mid: Tackle problems with limited existing solutions or success.
  - o High: Find new problems with few or no existing solutions.
- Fund research projects or testing of strategies and tactics.
- Allocate at least 20 per cent of your time to conduct research and tests, and codify ideas, methods, and results (this does not need to meet the level of traditional peer-reviewed scientific studies).

Now, people often get stuck on this pillar, arguing that everything has already been discovered, there's nothing new under the sun, and they have nothing unique to say. It's daunting to think that you need to put out visionary ideas, practices, or research! But you don't need to discover completely new information or share completely new ideas to be innovative and novel.

Instead, you can grow in this pillar in a few different ways. At the lowest level, you might focus on tactics from your own field and codifying tactics based on a tried-and-true strategy. As you grow, you might start adapting tactics from other fields into your workflows, building or innovating on others' research, and testing new strategies. You might also conduct original research or surveys on an existing problem to try to find new insights or update old information. At the top of the pillar, you're doing more rigorous research and publishing in academic journals or top-tier outlets, conducting independent research or using proprietary data to make connections across different problem spaces, and combining a mix of tactics and strategies from your own discipline and adjacent disciplines.

As you can see, depth of ideas is not just about net-new discoveries; it's about unique ways to find and articulate problems and find and implement solutions. Just because an idea or implementation has been shared before, does not mean that it has been said exactly as you would say it, implement it, or build on it, with your individual experience, expertise, and method of sharing. Your personal journey, processes, and outcomes make the ideas, strategies, and tactics unique, not necessarily whether the core concept has never been discussed.

It's not enough to simply do research or have novel ideas. In order to be a thought leader, you need to share these ideas with your audience. You must share your ideas in a way that allows others to engage, build on, and apply them in their own context. Thought leaders add to, not just change or disagree with, the existing conversation, best practices, and solutions. This is why simply saying the opposite of the current trend or best practice does not automatically make you a thought leader. You can be smart and impactful without being a thought leader. But to be a thought leader, you need to educate and empower others to achieve smarts and impact.

Given the importance of original research and codifying the process and outcomes in a way that others can follow, it's important to allow ample time for experimentation, measurement, and documentation. Many teams insist that they want internal subject matter experts to "do thought leadership," yet they don't give them time to actually take the steps required to come up with unique thoughts. Further, they don't give other teams the opportunity to learn from their peers, test the new concepts and tactics, and codify their insights as well. It's an anti-pattern to suggest that leaders or practitioners rush through a problem space or solution space to churn out content and call it thought leadership. True thought leadership takes time to develop, and requires resources to run experiments, conduct research, and vet outcomes.

Creating a Baseline Across the Four Pillars of Thought Leadership

The four pillars work together in tandem, and the goal is to move up in each pillar. I recommend scoring yourself or people you want to elevate in the organization in each pillar to create a baseline and measure progress towards becoming a thought leader. You could, for example, use red (beginner/poor), yellow (making progress but needs improvement), and green (successful) to indicate progress. (The following figures use dark, medium, and light shading in place of red, yellow, and green.)

Ideal Thought Leader Profile

In a perfect world, a true thought leader is strong in all four pillars, shown with the dark shading in the top boxes for each pillar in Figure 10.2. They are credible, with industry experts and outlets citing them as the source for an idea, strategy, or tactic. They have a strong profile, with name recognition and status. They are prolific, consistently writing and speaking in multiple formats, and regularly sharing and engaging on multiple platforms. They have a consistent depth of ideas that shape, change, and influence their industry and audience.

Figure 10.2   Ideal Thought Leader Profile

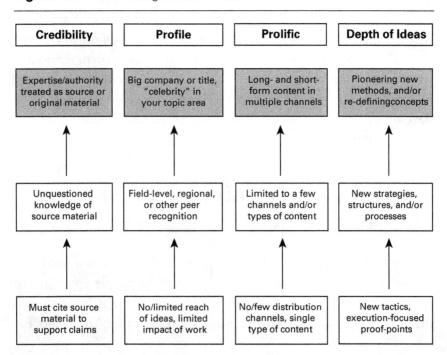

Unfortunately, the reality tends to be that reaching the highest level in each pillar is quite rare and, often, too daunting for someone who is just starting the journey. And, it's not helpful to simply strive for the highest level, without understanding the steps required to reach that level. For large organizations, you might find many people who are strong in one or two pillars, but lacking in the other pillars, which keeps them from being thought leaders.

By looking at the proof-points in each pillar and realistically scoring yourself or potential thought leaders, you can focus on implementing the tactics to grow in the pillars where you are weak. As highlighted earlier, there's no "most important" or "best" pillar. To be a thought leader, you need to be strong in all four pillars. So, it makes sense to focus more on weaker pillars if you're just starting your journey.

C-suite Profile

Many companies want to elevate their C-level executives or founders into thought leaders. As we noted in Chapter 9 when we defined thought leadership, this is often a struggle, particularly as these executives are too busy to ideate and share, and they don't want to be controversial or cause a panic among investors and shareholders by straying from the status quo. Figure 10.3 shows the baseline profile for a typical executive.

Executives tend to be strongest in the credibility pillar, since they have positional authority and a senior-level title, usually many years of experience in their industry or topic area, and the backing of the company (dark shading in the middle box of this pillar in Figure 10.3).

They're also making progress in the profile pillar, in large part because there are fewer executives in any industry or topic area, so most are known among their peers and competitors. Since these leaders tend to work in the same industry for many years, they've built a network by holding roles in multiple companies, or meeting with venture capitalists, private equity firms, and other investors to secure funding. Their current employees, job candidates, and past direct reports know them. These leaders tend to be invited to industry networking events or executive roundtables, which means they have a personal connection to many people in their network. However, they

Figure 10.3 C-suite Profile

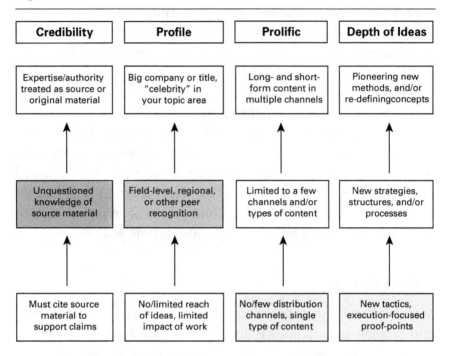

aren't well-known outside of their small circle, and they aren't building or growing a large external audience (medium gray shading in the middle box of the profile pillar in Figure 10.3).

Unfortunately, executives are generally weak in the prolific pillar and depth of ideas pillar. They don't dedicate time to research, experiments, or codifying their findings. This means that there aren't many new ideas or novel outcomes to fuel content creation, and they're too busy to sit down and write a long article, make time to shoot videos, or prepare and deliver sessions at a conference. They're not creating or sharing or engaging, which means they aren't influencing their audience or enabling them to take action. When they do share, it's primarily factual information, company-related statistics or news, or tried-and-true tactics the company already uses to produce steady outcomes (light shading for both the prolific pillar and the depth of ideas pillar).

Now, you might be thinking, "But executives work hard! They're smart! They're good at their job!", and this is true. But, remember, being good at your job does not make you a thought leader. Executives make an impact for the company and their career, but, if they're not shaping the industry by consistently sharing innovative ideas, and they're not building an external audience, they are not thought leaders.

In fact, C-suite leaders, executives, and founders are often not the best people to try to develop into thought leaders for an organization. It's not just because they're busy! It's because it's the opposite of what they're doing, day in and day out. Often, because execs spend so much time building consensus internally, they're a bit wary about sharing an opinionated point-of-view externally. They don't want to ruffle feathers with investors, recruiters, press, or any other key stakeholder internally or externally. They don't want to unleash an avalanche of potential negativity externally. Because of that, they come out with a watered-down perspective from public relations or marketing.

For something to be a piece of thought leadership, it must possess that leadership quality in terms of doing something new, helping people change direction, and helping people change their minds. Because that often causes a degree of controversy, it's uncomfortable to make that change. Folks in the C-suite struggle to share these disruptive ideas because they've been told in every other aspect of the business not to rock the boat. Thus, it's quite a mindset shift for many executives or founders to willingly share opinionated and differentiated ideas and perspectives.

Practitioner Profile

In contrast, Figure 10.4 shows the baseline profile for many smart, capable practitioners.

Practitioners have room for improvement in the credibility category, primarily because they don't have external credibility. These people are often the go-to subject-matter expert or execution person inside an organization, but, without positional authority or the halo of a strong company brand, their words don't carry the same weight as someone with a bigger title. The years of experience in the industry or problem space mean that seasoned practitioners have a lot of potential to grow quickly in this pillar, but they still need to prove that they possess expertise and experience if they try to share more externally (medium shading in the bottom box of the credibility pillar in Figure 10.4).

Figure 10.4   Practitioner Profile

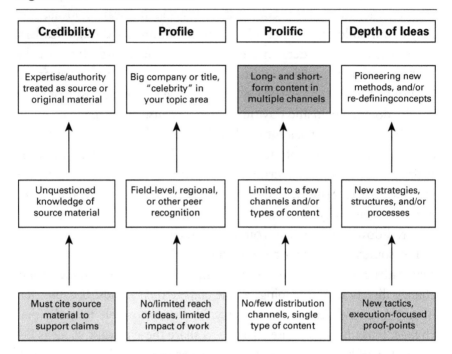

Practitioners are weakest in the profile pillar. They're not well-known, even in their industry niche, and their network primarily consists of current or former teammates or classmates. Even when companies try to put them forward for industry conferences or media requests, the organizer or journalist requests someone else. Their ideas yield little or no impact outside of their own team or organization, and their content doesn't get traction with external audiences (light shading in the bottom box of the profile pillar).

Perhaps surprisingly, practitioners tend to be quite prolific. They're talking, but they don't have a large audience listening. This is especially true in large organizations, where senior-level practitioners often write internal documentation or speak at internal meetings, such as town halls or learning sessions. They might post regularly on a small personal blog, Substack, or YouTube channel, but they have low monthly entrance counts and few subscribers. They might have plenty of ideas for conference sessions or articles, and they've created lots of content in personal channels. They're fluent in the skill of creating content, but, unfortunately, this content is locked in internal systems or niche corners of the internet (dark shading in the top box of the prolific pillar).

Practitioners also have potential to score well in depth of ideas, in large part because they're so familiar with the problem space. They can quickly come up with new tactics to solve problems, and they can identify adjacent problems and use their deep expertise to apply vetted tactics to the problem. In some cases, they're starting to move into creating new strategies, or helping other internal teams adapt solutions for adjacent problems. Given the time to experiment and codify their findings, practitioners have high potential to grow quickly in the depth of ideas pillar—it's usually resourcing constraints, not intellect or experience, that prevents them. Because they're so strong in the tactics, and often capable at developing and sharing new strategies, they score well (dark gray shading in the bottom box of the depth of ideas pillar).

In order for practitioners to grow into thought leaders, support from the organization is key. They benefit from the brand elevating them as spokespeople for external opportunities, funding new projects and exploration, and giving them time and a platform to codify and share their findings.

Realistic Thought Leader Profile

We've looked at the ideal thought leadership profile, executive profile, and practitioner profile, noting the challenges to reach the ideal state, and the weaknesses in specific pillars for different employees. So, what does a realistic thought leadership profile look like? What can companies expect if they put effort into helping leaders and practitioners improve their weaknesses? Let's take a look at the realistic thought leader profile.

As you can see in Figure 10.5, it's possible to grow in each pillar and score well across multiple pillars, without reaching the highest level. In order to be trusted, you need a minimum level of credibility and notoriety. In order to move the industry forward and enable your audience to take action, you need to have a minimum level of depth of ideas. The prolific pillar is the only one that does not rely on external perception or sentiment and is completely in the person's control. Therefore, you *do* need to aim for the highest level to be strong in this pillar.

Figure 10.5   Realistic Thought Leader Profile

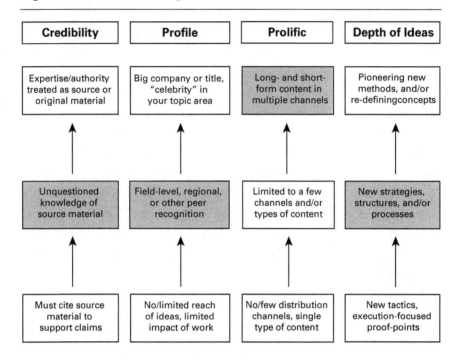

THOUGHT LEADER
Nancy Duarte

Nancy Duarte is a storytelling expert and CEO of Duarte, Inc., a communication training and creative presentation agency. Nancy is well-known in the tech and communication industries, and her company has worked with some of the biggest names in Silicon Valley, including Apple, Adobe, Amazon, and Salesforce. She ranks well in all four pillars (Figure 10.6).

   Let's take a look at why she is so strong in each pillar. Remember, some of these proof-points count towards ranking well in multiple pillars, since the pillars work together in tandem to measure a thought leader.

Credibility: Nancy has been working in business storytelling and presentation training since 1988, and her agency client roster and personal appearances on stages, podcasts, and in publications show that she's an expert, with lived experience.

Figure 10.6   Thought Leader Nancy Duarte's Profile

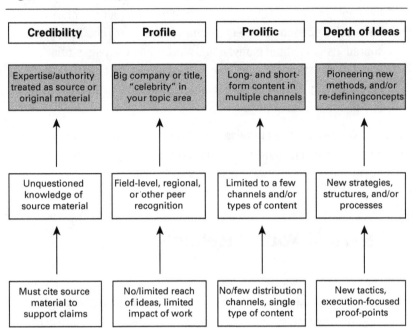

Credibility	Profile	Prolific	Depth of Ideas
Expertise/authority treated as source or original material	Big company or title, "celebrity" in your topic area	Long- and short-form content in multiple channels	Pioneering new methods, and/or re-definingconcepts
↑	↑	↑	↑
Unquestioned knowledge of source material	Field-level, regional, or other peer recognition	Limited to a few channels and/or types of content	New strategies, structures, and/or processes
↑	↑	↑	↑
Must cite source material to support claims	No/limited reach of ideas, limited impact of work	No/few distribution channels, single type of content	New tactics, execution-focused proof-points

Profile: Nancy has spoken on large stages, such as TEDx, published with prestigious publications, including *Harvard Business Review* (HBR), and has gained over 200,000 followers on LinkedIn and over 52,000 on X.

Prolific: Nancy has been publishing and speaking since 2008, when her first book, *Slide:ology*, hit the shelves. Since then, she's authored and co-authored an additional five books and numerous articles, and delivered talks in person and virtually. She shares regularly on LinkedIn and X. She continues to speak at conferences, and she features regularly as a guest on popular podcasts, including *Lenny's Podcast*. She's also a frequent byline and speaker on Duarte-owned channels, and her books are the foundation of multiple Duarte training courses.

Depth of ideas: In her book, *Resonate*, Nancy details her discovery of the shape of persuasive talks. After analyzing talks that galvanized movements, sold millions of units of products, and acted as the catalyst for organizational transformation, she discovered key patterns that they all had in common. She shared these insights in her book and in her TEDx talk, showing the "frequency" of a persuasive speech.[2] Since then, she's researched, codified, and shared insights about motivational stories and warning stories during a transformation journey, tactical tips to pair persuasive presentations with detailed documents, and how to use data to gain buy-in and create change.

In sum, Nancy continues to raise the bar on persuasive communication via ongoing insights, shared in different formats and channels, with real impact to show for those who consume and implement her ideas.

Understand Your Baseline

Now that you understand the four pillars of credibility, profile, prolific, and depth of ideas, you can create a baseline for yourself or the colleagues you're trying to help become thought leaders. As noted in the details of each pillar, the proof-points for each level in each pillar are meant to be guidelines. You need to do some research in your space to understand what number of followers, number/mix of channels, and types of assets, conferences, and podcasts are relevant for your niche.

Take an honest inventory of where you stand for each pillar. How many social media followers do you have across all of your platforms? How often do you write and speak? What is the nature of the outlets where you publish and speak? These answers create the baseline across each of the four pillars and give you an indication of where to focus your efforts.

I'm often asked, "Which pillar is the hardest?" I believe this is the wrong question, and highly dependent on the potential thought leader's skills, interest, and current momentum. For example, many marketers assume that depth of ideas is the most difficult pillar. They're already fluent in the skill of writing, speaking, publishing, and engaging on social media, and building an audience across multiple platforms. Thus, for many marketers and communication professionals, coming up with differentiated, opinionated, and actionable insights is the most difficult part. In contrast, many people who come from more technical professions, like software engineering, struggle with the prolific and profile pillars. They're not in the habit of writing and speaking publicly, they rarely share or engage on social media, and they're not sure how to go about securing more external opportunities to share their ideas. Again, this reinforces the idea that all four pillars work together in tandem, and a thought leader is strong in all four pillars. Simply publishing often does not make you a thought leader. Simply doing great work does not make you a thought leader.

The baseline helps you understand where you need to focus your efforts, and offers recommendations on how to spend your time. For example, in the case of the marketer or communications professional who is already comfortable creating and sharing regularly, they need more time to run experiments and codify their findings. It's not the sharing that's difficult; it's the ability to zoom out to find the patterns that form the frameworks, which become the basis of the depth of ideas required to be a thought leader. They often benefit from pairing with colleagues or peers who are strong in research, data modeling, and pattern recognition.

The opposite is true for people who are not in the habit of sharing externally, but have a backlog of ideas or partial talks, frameworks, and articles. In their case, they benefit from either pairing with a marketing or communications professional, or taking writing, social media, and public speaking courses. They need help ideating multiple angles for their core ideas, thinking about how to match narratives with assets and channels, and understanding the requirements to secure speaking engagements and contributed bylines.

Again, there's no "best" pillar or "right" place to start. The key is to conduct an honest assessment of your current state, and then focus your attention on the weakest pillar(s).

Now, I understand that some people might score poorly in all four pillars. This is particularly common for people who are early in their career or less experienced in their profession. In this case, I recommend a different course of action, depending on the reason for the low baseline assessment:

- **Early-career professional:** This person likely lacks credibility as the core problem. When you're early in your career, you don't possess credentials, years of experience, or proof of progress to enhance your credibility. In this case, partnering with someone with a stronger baseline score helps improve the position. Of course, this assumes that the person in question does have smart ideas, is doing impactful work, and is willing to start consistently sharing on external platforms. It's also worth starting small, publishing on a personal or company blog, speaking at industry meet-ups, and doing meaningful work in your career to improve.

- **Mid-to-late-career professional:** This person tends to be low in the prolific and profile pillars as the core problem. Because they've been working for a while, they have credibility via years of experience, and likely have decent depth of ideas if they were to sit down and codify them. Here, I recommend focusing on the prolific pillar. This person benefits from publishing consistently in at least one channel and one asset type. The specific channel and format are less important than building the habit and skill to publish regularly. Because these people are close to the problem and solution space, the act of creating and sharing helps them find the patterns and systems and hone their ideas into something that's useful to the rest of the world. They use the task of writing or filming on a regular schedule to refine their ideas and voice.

QUICK TIPS TO GET STARTED WITH THOUGHT LEADERSHIP

To get started on your journey to becoming a thought leader, consider the following quick ideas:

- Use the baseline profile exercise to determine where you need to focus. If you're low in all areas, start with the prolific pillar, followed by the depth of ideas pillar. Get in the habit of publishing regularly, starting with two prompts: a question I asked today, and a question I answered today. These give you a starting point that is grounded in your day-to-day reality, and helps you start to see patterns in your perceived areas of expertise. Creating regularly helps codify your expertise, and gives you content to start sharing, which contributes to being prolific and increasing your credibility.

- Just publish. Seriously! Perfect is the enemy of done, so start sharing. For most B2B professionals, LinkedIn is the place to be. It works well with the two prompts in the previous bullet, focusing on real-world experience and scenarios. You can dive into the comments on the post and engage in comments on other people's posts.

- Create the foundational assets for pitching. Most outlets require a short bio (usually under 100 words, sometimes as few as 50 words) and an abstract (usually fewer than 300 words, sometimes under 150 words). Take a nice headshot with decent lighting and an uncluttered background. It makes it much easier to submit for a guest blog or conference slot when you have these assets ready to go.

We'll explore in-depth exercises in the following chapters, but everyone has to start somewhere. If you want to start improving your baseline profile or building thought leaders in your company, the first step is to start sharing.

Conclusion

Thought leaders help build trust and enable their audience to take action in a new direction. In order to be a thought leader, someone must be strong in the four pillars of credibility, profile, prolific, and depth of ideas. Each pillar is important, and all four reinforce each other.

Being **credible** means that people believe what you say as an expert in your specialty. You can demonstrate credibility through years of experience, formal credentials, and regularly sharing insights on your discipline and industry.

A strong **profile** means you're well-known in your field and industry. You've built a large, engaged audience who follow you on social media, attend your presentations, and consume and amplify your work.

Being **prolific** means that you share insights regularly, in multiple formats and channels. This pillar is the only one that is completely in your control, so it's important to establish habits that allow you to create and share consistently.

Having a **depth of ideas** differentiates thought leaders from influencers and subject-matter experts (SMEs). Strength in this pillar means that you codify and share novel ideas. You apply new tactics and strategies to achieve outsized results, and share those insights in a way that helps your audience take action.

In the following chapters, we'll talk about how to work with different types of creators along the journey, and ultimately, build thought leaders in your organization.

Chapter Summary

- The four pillars of thought leadership are credibility, profile, prolific, and depth of ideas. Thought leaders are strong in all four pillars.

- Create a baseline across all four pillars to understand where to focus in order to grow as a thought leader. Think holistically about the potential of people across the organization, and help executives and practitioners grow in pillars where they are weak.

- Codifying and sharing insights regularly and building and engaging with the audience helps aspiring thought leaders grow in each pillar.

Notes

1 Newport, C. (2025) Meet Cal Newport, calnewport.com (archived at https://perma.cc/6DVM-2GPJ)

2 Duarte (2025) Our Story, duarte.com/why-duarte/our-story (archived at https://perma.cc/G4DA-HJC5)

Evolve the   11
Marketing Mix

Influencers, Subject-Matter Experts, and Thought Leaders

Thought leaders are important individuals to help companies build trust and affinity with their audiences, but they are not the only type of creator who can add value to the marketing mix. Influencers and subject-matter experts offer more ways to expand your bench of partners and spokespeople.

As we saw in Chapter 10 on the pillars of thought leadership, it takes a lot of work to become a true thought leader. Thus, many marketing and communications professionals want to find an easier way to create content, attract and engage an audience, and build a bench of spokespeople.

With the rise of the creator economy, there are more opportunities to work with individuals across a variety of topics, skills, and channels, resulting in questions such as:

- What are the differences between an influencer, subject-matter expert, or thought leader?
- Which type of creator is the best fit for my marketing mix?
- Does it even matter which type of creator we choose?

During this chapter, we'll explore the differences between these creators, along with strategies and tactics to incorporate them into your marketing plans.

Profile Assessments: Influencer, Subject-Matter Expert, and Thought Leader

First, is there a difference between a thought leader, a subject-matter expert (SME), and an influencer? In short, yes! Let's use the four-pillar framework to assess each type of creator. As a reminder, the assessment pillars are credibility, profile, prolific, and depth of ideas.

Influencers (profiled in Figure 11.1) tend to be well-known, but they're not really creating any new ideas. They're early adopters, they're well-spoken, they're gregarious, and thus, people listen to them. With the rise of social media, many influencers are similar to minor celebrities (think Instagram lifestyle or travel influencers). B2B influencers do exist too, and they're growing in popularity. They don't usually have an "influencer" title, instead having titles like champion, evangelist, ambassador, partner, and in some cases, advisor. (Advisor roles don't necessarily indicate that someone acts as an influencer on behalf of a brand; but, for people with a large, engaged following on social media, taking an advisory role often includes promoting the company on their personal social media channels.)

Subject-matter experts (Figure 11.2) possess a lot of knowledge. They've worked in the industry for a long time, experienced all facets of a specific problem, and thus can often propose new solutions and move their team and company forward. However, many SMEs don't understand personal branding, or how to create multiple types of content and consistently share externally. This is particularly true of people in more technical disciplines. I've worked with many smart engineers, but they aren't well-known beyond their tight circle, and they don't put their ideas and knowledge out into the world unprompted. Think about your go-to person internally. How many people externally know them as the go-to person?

Thought leaders are strong in all four pillars (Figure 11.3). They have experience and knowledge. They are well-known. They share often and in a variety of channels and formats. They're pushing the conversation forward, making an impact by adding new elements, and shaping how the next generation solves problems.

Figure 11.1   Influencer Profile

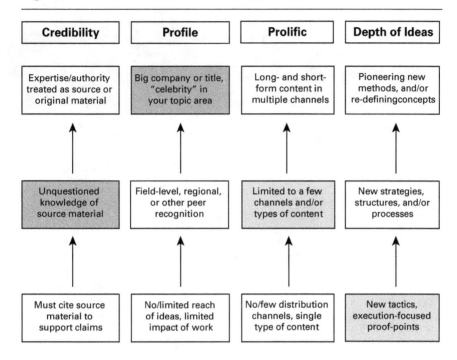

Figure 11.2   Subject-Matter Expert Profile

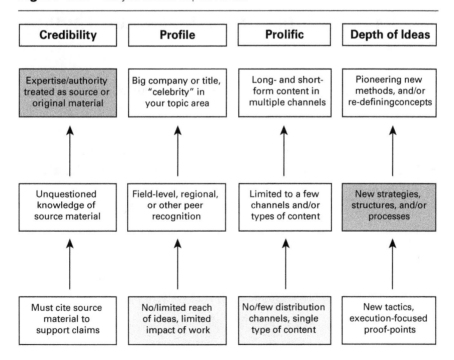

Figure 11.3 Thought Leader Profile

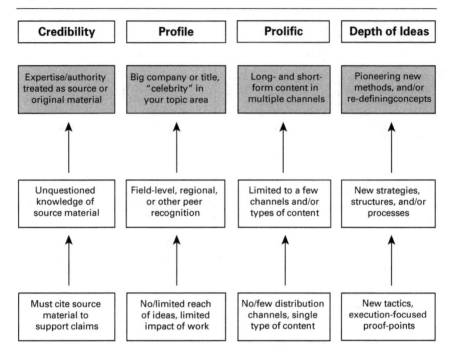

The Value of Influencers, SMEs, and Thought Leaders

Let's consider the next two questions often asked: Which type of creator is the best fit for my marketing programs, and does it matter which type of creator we choose? To be clear, all three types of creators are valuable, but they're not the same. Companies need a mix of influencers, SMEs, and thought leaders, but each offers a slightly different value.

Let's take a look at how each creator fits into the marketing mix:

- **Influencers tend to help you reach a new audience.** The key here is that you need to build a long-term partnership, not a short-term advertisement. The reason these people have credibility with your ideal audience is because they *don't* sell. If you want a spokesperson who follows a script, you're running an ad campaign, not an influencer program. Influencers do have credibility with their audience, but their personal brand and ability to create engaging content tends to stand out more than their ideas. Influencers help drive short-term awareness goals and long-term sales goals.

- **Subject-matter experts help you explain how to solve problems, troubleshoot, and educate on existing solutions.** In many cases, they focus primarily on internal employees, existing customers or users, and the existing audience. For example, SMEs frequently present at company-sponsored user conferences or write articles for the company blog. They can have influence externally, but two big differentiators for SMEs compared to thought leaders is the size of their external audience and depth of ideas. SMEs help drive medium- and long-term usage goals.

- **Thought leaders focus on new ideas in the market.** They drive the conversation about what's next, and they help the audience think in a new way. They have credibility and influence with internal and external audiences, including audiences outside of the existing user base. They're talking about new problems, new solutions, and new strategies and tactics. Thought leaders help educate the market and build trust for the company, and help drive long-term impact for sales, partnerships, recruiting, investing, and affinity goals.

Each creator offers a different type of impact in the marketing mix. The following are some questions to consider as you look at working with different types of creators:

- What do you mean by "impact"?
  - o As a marketer, most of my goals and metrics focus on attracting new customers, retaining existing customers, and growing product use among those groups via retention, cross-sell, and up-sell campaigns.
  - o As a recruiting team, your goals focus on attracting quality talent.
  - o As an investor relations team, your goals focus on inspiring confidence in the market to improve the stock price.
  - o Other teams throughout the organization might focus on different goals and metrics.
  - o "Impact" is not one-size-fits-all, so, start by outlining the outcomes you want to achieve.

- Who are your audience members, and what are their pain-points? Are they internal or external, practitioners or executives?
    - Different creators solve different problems for different audiences.
    - Their credibility and depth of ideas are key differentiators when choosing which creator to match to each problem.
- What gaps in content do you have, and what capabilities do you have in-house?
    - If you already have strong internal thought leaders who produce and share content regularly, you might need to focus more on partnering with an influencer to reach a new audience.
    - If all of your content is locked in internal channels, you might need to help your SMEs start sharing externally.
    - If you have lots of other people talking about you, but little original content coming from an internal spokesperson, you might need to focus on building up thought leaders in the organization.
    - The gaps and capabilities assessment helps you understand which type of creator might be missing from your bench.

As you can see in Figure 11.4, each type of creator offers different value and impact in the marketing mix. One is not "better" than another, and you need to bring in the right balance of people, based on your strategy, tactics, and goals.

Figure 11.4   Comparing B2B Creators

Creator Type	Primary Audience	Ideas	Metrics	Time Horizon
Influencer	External	Existing solutions	Awareness and sales	Short-term and long-term
Subject-Matter Expert (SME)	Internal	Existing problems and solutions	Usage	Medium- and long-term
Thought Leader	Internal and external	New problems and solutions	Trust and affinity	Long-term

Working with Influencers

Influencer marketing is on the rise, with the Influencer Marketing Hub estimated that it would grow to $24 billion by the end of 2024.[1]

The term "influencer" is quite broad. With the rise of the general creator economy, it can mean everything from a B2C (business-to-consumer) account promoting beauty products, clothing, and travel destinations on Instagram, to an independent video game player who live streams on Twitch or YouTube, to an industry heavyweight who pens white papers for B2B audiences.

When we think about influencers in relation to the four-pillar framework, we're focusing on B2B influencers, not B2C or personalities with a large following on a few social media channels. Similar to the guidelines noted when discussing thought leadership, the influencers discussed in this chapter are not celebrities or famous people, they're knowledge workers with B2B expertise and offerings.

B2B influencers are strongest in the profile pillar, with a decent amount of credibility. However, they tend to focus on a small number of channels and asset types. It's common for a B2B influencer to grow their follower count on LinkedIn or X, focusing primarily on short- or mid-form text. They may also have a strong presence on YouTube, creating mid-form educational videos.

Common Mistakes in Influencer Marketing

Focusing on the Largest Following

In the past, brands looking to partner with an influencer wanted someone with the largest following. The goal was to blast the brand message to as many people as possible, with the belief that the person with the most followers makes the most effective influencer. Unfortunately, many of these followers are not buyers or decision-makers for the company's offering. Simply having a lot of followers does not mean that an influencer can monetize that following.

Instead, companies need to look at the make-up of the influencer's audience to decide whether their content is likely to resonate with that audience. Nano- and micro-influencers might be better partners for companies with a niche audience and specific ideal customer profile (ICP). What counts as a nano-, micro-, macro-, or celebrity-level influencer varies by industry, so do your research into whether the audience includes the right people, and whether they're engaged or just focusing on follower count.

Consider the channel too. Many influencers are strong in one or two channels, and it can be advantageous to partner with someone who is strong in a channel where the overall brand presence is weak. For example, if your brand handles are strong on LinkedIn and X, you could reach a new audience by partnering with an influencer who has a large subscriber base on YouTube. Or, in contrast, you might choose to invest more in a channel where you're strong, to give the appearance of a channel takeover. This strategy is particularly effective when paired with an employee advocacy program and ad spend. By concentrating your efforts into a single channel, your audience believes that you're "everywhere" because they see employees posting about the brand, influencers posting about the brand, and your branded ads and branded posts.

Forcing Influencers to Promote Company-Approved Content

I'm often asked how to get an influencer to promote the company, using copy and images provided by marketing. My answer is that you don't!

Influencers build their audience using their authentic voice and unique style of creating and sharing content. If they suddenly change their content to blatantly promotional brand content, they lose the trust and rapport they have built with the audience.

Instead, focus on influencers who already align with your brand values and overall brand personality so that you can trust them to create generally brand-aligned content on their own. Properly vetted influencers don't need a verbatim script because they already intuitively speak in a way that aligns with the brand and resonates with the target audience. If you feel that you need to micromanage the content creation process, you're probably not working with the right influencer for your company.

Short-Term, Transactional Engagement

Similar to the pitfall just noted, it's a mistake to treat influencers as one-off spokespeople for a short-lived campaign. Again, if you want to hire someone to read a script for an ad, that's a different set of use cases and outcomes than partnering with an influencer.

Just as influencers build a relationship with their audience, brands need to build relationships with their influencers. Working with a small cohort of long-term influencer partners helps the influencer create better content on behalf of the brand and helps the influencer's audience build trust with the brand over time.

An ad looks and sounds like a sales pitch because that's precisely what it is! It's pure buy-intent content, meant to drive short-term conversion. In contrast, influencers can share content with multiple intents, including use intent, help intent, and learn intent. Ideally, the influencer is already familiar with your offering and genuinely believes it's helpful and worth the money.

In fact, customers and users can be a great pool of influencer partners for this reason. As we saw in Chapter 8 on the power of community, many companies have built large, passionate user communities. These people already have a relationship with the brand, and they would be very happy to develop a more formal partnership for sharing content about the company and its offerings.

External influencers generally require monetary compensation for their work, although most are in it for more than money, while users, customers, and employees might have different motives for sharing branded content. Instead of assuming that every type of influencer requires a brand deal worth thousands of dollars, tailor the incentives to each cohort. If you host a user conference, it might include presenting a session, solidifying the user as a premier expert in your products. For employees, sharing on behalf of the company might help them make the case for a promotion, a move into a different team, or a career change with a different skillset.

Don't skimp on the budget to compensate influencers, but don't forget that there are many ways to exchange value, and each influencer is different in what makes them feel rewarded, recognized, and valued.

Focusing Solely on External Influencers

Most companies think that influencer marketing is about hiring an external person to promote the company and its offerings, but employees can also be influencers.

External influencers have credibility and knowledge to share authentically with their audience, and it's the same for employees. They should be building their own audience, based on their unique expertise and experience, and fostering long-term relationships. Of course, that tends to intersect with the company or offering, since they wouldn't choose to work for the company if they didn't believe in the offerings, and they likely regularly solve customer problems as part of their job.

WHAT TO LOOK FOR WHEN YOU BUILD A PARTNERSHIP WITH INFLUENCERS AND EMPLOYEES

Values

Start here! Do you fundamentally agree on core values? If you want to hire influencers or employees to represent your brand, they need to genuinely believe in the core values.

Passion for Creating and Sharing

I've stopped trying to convince people to create and share if they don't want to. It's a losing battle. If someone is only doing it because they're forced to for their job, the content will be lackluster.

This is also true for influencer partnerships. Find someone who is already excited about your space and your offering. If they already talk about the brand, that's a much better starting point (even if their audience is smaller) than paying them to talk about a one-off feature.

Content Skills

I'm less concerned about the specific asset or channel, but you must find people who are already capable of creating content. Don't try to force employees who dislike public speaking, are slow or poor writers, and who don't have a regular practice of creating content on social media to become evangelists.

Influencers became influencers precisely because they were able to create content that an audience wants to consume. So, let them have creative freedom to share! Remember, you already align on values, and you're building a long-term partnership, so don't try to force specific assets or channels when you partner with an influencer.

Internal Influencers Versus External Influencers

Internal and external influencers share several common traits:

- Both have credibility with their audience.
- Both have strong and recognizable personal brands.
- Both create and share content consistently.

However, each type of influencer offers different value to the business. The biggest difference between internal and external influencers is, of course, that internal influencers are employees of the company, while external influencers are not.

To be clear, internal influencers are not the same as an employee advocate or amplification program. These people have already built a strong personal brand and shown they can grow an audience of their own in at least one channel. The marketing or communications team tends to run employee advocacy programs, with goals around amplifying company-related content and campaigns, and generally prescribing or providing content for employees to share en masse.

In contrast, internal influencers naturally weave the company-related and role-related content into their existing editorial calendar, and they use their practical experience to share broader expertise. They're rarely willing to copy and paste content provided by another team, and they've honed an audience that relates to their core expertise, not just the target audience that the company wants to reach. Internal influencers are generally associated with the company, and often start building their personal brand using the company narratives or reputation as a halo.

In some cases, companies might build these people up to be the "face" of the brand, but only after the employee has already built their own audience. This is a tricky balance, because internal influencers lose credibility if they start sounding like an ad for the product or brand in every post.

As we saw in Chapter 7 on the new rules of social media, brands should create a symbiotic relationship with internal influencers. They shouldn't try to co-opt an employee's personal brand and audience trust solely for the benefit of the brand. Instead, they should partner with the internal influencer to boost their content and visibility on paid, owned, and earned channels.

INTERNAL INFLUENCER
Laura Erdem from Dreamdata

Laura Erdem is a sales leader at Dreamdata, a B2B attribution software company. She's also an internal influencer. Figure 11.5 shows how Laura scores across the four pillars.

Laura shares content about attribution in the buyer's journey, as well as tips and tactics for salespeople who want to use LinkedIn to reach their sales quotas. Because she has worked in sales for over a decade and risen through the ranks from a junior sales representative to managing an entire region, Laura has strong credibility with her audience of sales representatives. In addition, given that she frequently

Figure 11.5   Internal Influencer Laura Erdem's Profile

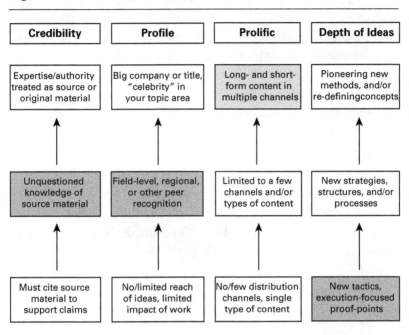

Credibility	Profile	Prolific	Depth of Ideas
Expertise/authority treated as source or original material	Big company or title, "celebrity" in your topic area	Long- and short-form content in multiple channels	Pioneering new methods, and/or re-definingconcepts
Unquestioned knowledge of source material	Field-level, regional, or other peer recognition	Limited to a few channels and/or types of content	New strategies, structures, and/or processes
Must cite source material to support claims	No/limited reach of ideas, limited impact of work	No/few distribution channels, single type of content	New tactics, execution-focused proof-points

needs to present about pipeline, revenue forecasts, and deal cycles, she's a user of the Dreamdata product she sells, which also gives her credibility with the ideal customer profile (ICP) she wants to reach.

Laura has over 30,000 followers on LinkedIn, and her posts consistently receive comments and reactions from her followers. She speaks at in-person and virtual conferences and she appears as a guest on webinars and podcasts, so her profile continues to grow.

Like many influencers, Laura is not as active on multiple channels or multiple asset types. She shares regularly on LinkedIn, generally posting a mix of text articles and short- or mid-form videos.

Most of the information Laura shares focuses on new tactics, primarily with her approach to LinkedIn. Her success in building an audience and generating leads for Dreamdata led the rest of the Dreamdata team to test LinkedIn. They set a goal for the team to generate millions of impressions in a quarter on LinkedIn, and shared a behind-the-scenes look at how experts like Laura helped the team improve their presence and content.

> She also regularly shares product demos, a look at her dashboard for deal cycles, and how the Dreamdata team shows up at industry events. Laura's signature hats and matching team outfits connect her personal brand strongly to the company brand.

In contrast, external influencers are not heavily associated with the brand, and don't work directly for the company. Their primary expertise aligns to the industry and the target audience, not the company or its offerings.

Note that external influencers are different from the ambassadors that we discussed in Chapter 8, as ambassadors regularly share content that relates to and champions a brand. They might be users or partners, but they're highly associated with the brand and its offerings, and brand-related content represents a key element in their content mix.

External influencers tend to build their audience by sharing industry- or craft-related content. They talk about overall industry trends and best practices, and details about what it's like to work in their role or career. They might have partnerships with multiple brands, and they often start as power-users of the product or service. This gives them credibility with both the audience and the company, while helping to maintain the sense of neutrality and not selling too heavily.

External influencers often have a well-known narrative style or signature type of content that they share, so they're unlikely to share company-provided assets that don't fit their overall content strategy and style—which is ok! Because they're expert creators who know what resonates with their audience, companies partnering with external influencers should *collaborate* on the content, not dictate the content.

EXTERNAL INFLUENCER
Sara Stella Lattanzio

Sara is the head of marketing at Stryber and an expert content strategist. She's also an external influencer, partnering with brands like Semrush and RivalFlow AI. Figure 11.6 shows how Sara scores across the four pillars.

Sara has been working in marketing, with a focus in content marketing for over 10 years, and has been sharing about her challenges and insights for several years on LinkedIn. It's clear that Sara knows content strategy inside and out, so she has strong credibility with content marketers and other specialists who work in adjacent disciplines, like SEO and social media.

Sara is all-in on LinkedIn, and has grown to having over 43,000 followers. She also occasionally appears as a guest on podcasts or events. She's an expert at creating short videos and carousels on LinkedIn, with a strong visual brand that shows up across her posts.

In the depth of ideas pillar, Sara consistently shares practical strategies and tactics to improve content marketing efforts, and she's starting to share new strategies to apply the latest artificial intelligence tools, capabilities, and use cases.

Figure 11.6   External Influencer Sara Stella Lattanzio's Profile

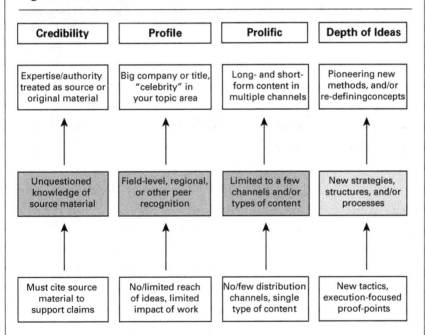

She regularly incorporates paid posts from her influencer partnerships into her content, but, because she's already a user of the products, and their core audience overlaps with her audience, the content doesn't feel

like a thinly veiled sales pitch. These influencer posts receive a lot of engagement, on par with many of her non-paid posts, precisely because they're aligned to the content she already shares, and her examples showcase how she would actually use the tool or feature in her day-to-day work.

For example, she often creates carousels with screenshots from the product, including her tips and tricks to gain more insights by using the featured capabilities. She introduces the problem at the beginning, and then boldly introduces the tool as part of the solution. She also contrasts the old way of solving the problem with the new way, so that the audience learns something, whether they use the featured tool or not. Then, she connects the dots about how to implement the solution, showcasing the strategy, tactics, and helpful features of the tool.

Sara is such an effective external influencer because she's talking about products that she genuinely uses and shows the value that she personally receives from the brands she works with. Her followers are an exact match for the company's ICP, and the brand content she shares is an exact match for their challenges.

Pairing Marketers with SMEs and Aspiring Thought Leaders

As noted in Chapter 9 where we defined thought leadership, people often ask me about working with a ghostwriter, and, with the rise in AI capabilities, whether someone can use AI and still be a thought leader. My answer may surprise you: It's yes! You can work with a ghostwriter or use AI and still be a thought leader.

Unfortunately, many people don't truly intend to partner with a ghostwriter or use AI for brainstorming or editing. Instead, they want someone to come up with ideas, do all the research, all the writing, all the editing, all the publishing, all the distribution, and all the engagement.

That's now how thought leadership works. Thought leadership requires the individual to have thoughts and be a leader! You can't outsource the thinking. Coming up with the ideas and angles via the brainstorming and category mapping exercise detailed in Chapter 12 on building thought leaders is an essential step in helping you grow in the depth of ideas and prolific pillars required for thought leadership.

This is why marketers are excellent partners for SME, particularly those who want to grow into thought leaders. The marketer uses their expertise to *help* find, understand, and build an audience, hone the SME's expertise into a narrative, and ensure that the content created by the SME is distributed according to best practices for each platform. It requires a consistent partnership, not a transactional relationship where the SME tosses a raw idea over to a marketer to turn into a usable asset, only to slap the SME's name on it before sharing it with the world.

For ghostwriting to work, the writer needs someone to "ghost." The term implies that someone was once alive and well and their spirit lives on in the form of the ghost. This same concept applies to aspiring thought leaders and potential marketing or communications partners. Once the thought leader creates a significant body of source material, a writer or video editor can turn it into modular content to extend the shelf life and reach. Thought leadership content becomes another set of assets to decompose or rebuild into a new asset to extend the playground as we discussed in Chapter 4, but it doesn't change the core ideas that the thought leader originated and codified.

USING AI TO CREATE CONTENT

I'd be remiss to ignore the role of emerging AI technology and tools. AI capabilities are changing rapidly, and many individuals and companies are incorporating AI-powered tools into their workflows.

To be clear, asking a large language model (LLM) to generate content that requires deep industry or product expertise or new, innovative ideas, is a losing tactic. Humans must come up with the original ideas and source material. However, AI can help streamline the process of turning those ideas and source material into multiple formats and assets. It can also help during the ideation process, and, with careful priming and prompting, can create robust long-form content.

The following are easy ways to start using AI as part of your content creation process:

- **Video editing**: Take a long video of a webinar or live presentation and upload it to an AI-assisted editing tool. The tool quickly creates shorter clips from the video. A human reviewer can choose the best clips and adjust them as needed for use on social media, landing pages, and other marketing outlets.

- **Summarizing customer questions or support tickets**: If you're looking for ways to make your content relevant to your audience, it's imperative that you know which questions they ask and where they struggle when they use your product or services. AI tools that summarize sales calls, support tickets, and customer reference conversations help you find the most pressing questions to answer for your audience. A human can write expert answers, or pair with AI to combine and edit source material into easy-to-find and easy-to-consume content. For example, a human might ask AI to summarize multiple pages of technical documentation into a skimmable FAQ format. The human uses their expertise to curate relevant source material, the AI uses compute power to synthesize the long-form content, and the human finishes with their skills in editing for accuracy and readability.

- **Generating presentation slides or other visual assets**: Many design software providers have added AI capabilities to their tools, allowing non-designers to easily create slides that adhere to the brand's visual identity. Marketers or SMEs can upload a page of notes to the tool, shape the prompt to include presentation length, brand guidelines, and other relevant information, and the AI design tool delivers a first draft of the slides.

New AI tools hit the market daily, so keep an open mind about how to pair humans and AI to make content creation and adaptation more efficient. Remember, the goal is *not* to use AI to churn out a huge volume of generic content, but rather to augment the skills and workflows in the team.

The following recommendations help to ensure that you build a true partnership with your SMEs:

- **Empower the SME creator to personalize the content and use their own voice.** Part of the reason the audience wants to hear from the SME is because they're the expert. They have credibility because they possess deep knowledge of the problem space, and they offer practical, actionable advice on implementing solutions. This expertise and insight are obscured when marketers turn it into a thinly veiled sales pitch instead of helping the SME find and share in their own voice. Further, consider how many rounds of editing and revision are required if the SME says, "It just doesn't sound like 'me'!" By helping the creator hone their own voice, you eliminate unnecessary rounds of feedback.

- **Teach the creator how to think about slicing and dicing their own content.** Many smart people with deep expertise in their chosen discipline aren't fluent in the skill of creating modular content. They think they need to tell the entire story in every single asset. This is time-consuming and leads to boredom or burnout. Instead, use the tactics noted in Chapter 4 on increasing the reach and impact of content to help the content creator find new ways to tell their story and share their expertise. Help them understand how to address topics at different depths, and how to adapt narratives into different asset types, as discussed in Chapter 3.

- **Allow marketing to scale by distributing the repurposing work.** When creators become more self-sufficient, it frees up the marketers to tackle more complex marketing problems and pursue marketing-related goals. Thought leadership is not meant to drive short-term revenue, and it's only one element of a comprehensive content strategy. Thus, marketers who train their aspiring thought leaders on the basics of content creation, distribution, and repackaging and repurposing will have more time to focus on activities that drive short- and medium-term revenue.

Not all SMEs want to become influencers or thought leaders, but they still provide value in the marketing mix. The key differentiator between SMEs and the other types of creators is their ability and desire to consistently create and share externally. So, how can you partner with SMEs who don't want to dedicate time to grow in the profile and prolific pillars?

Internal Reviews and Editorial Contributions

Because they possess extensive knowledge and experience in their field, SMEs are excellent reviewers for technical content, and might be open to having a byline or editorial contribution for content that an agency or marketing partner creates. The goal is not that they rubber stamp marketing content, but they pair to help reach a technical audience.

This is particularly helpful for expanding on content created to help drive organic traffic. With the rise of AI, many companies turn to these tools to pump out a large volume of articles to top the SERPs, steal traffic from their competitors, and significantly increase their organic traffic. However, purely AI-generated content is often generic, and lacks the depth of a true expert.

By partnering with SMEs to infuse expertise and actual experience, marketers can transform these articles into deep, useful pieces of content for the audience. Further, with Google's algorithm updates to bring in more human expertise, naming a SME as an editorial contributor or bylined writer helps enhance the credibility of the article.

Customer Engagements

Depending on the organization, SMEs might sit in the customer success or solution engineering teams. They have deep knowledge of the problem space, they're experts in the solution space, and they've usually spent a portion of their career creating products, processes, and systems to solve those problems. Customers and prospects love to speak with them because they faced the problem and successfully implemented solutions.

It's a common misconception that, just because SMEs don't want to be highly visible on social media, it means they are shy, scared of presenting, or otherwise unwilling to share their ideas. This is incorrect. Many SMEs love talking with customers and helping them work through difficult problems, so don't overlook them for sales or customer-facing roles.

Sales Training and Demo Creation

As just noted, many SMEs thrive on helping users solve problems and equipping their teammates to help customers solve problems. In more technical industries, they often enjoy building and showcasing solutions. Ask your SMEs to help build demo versions of the product, create demo videos or decks to share on company-owned properties, and book time for them to help train the sales team.

Presenting at Company-Hosted Events

Because of their credibility with the target audience and deep expertise in the company's products or services, SMEs can be an excellent choice for user conferences, webinars, and virtual events. They can use nearly identical decks that they create for sales training or customer meetings, along with product environments that they create for demos, to present at in-person conferences or on-demand webinars. The reach of these engagements is usually limited to prospective or existing customers, and the narrative is highly aligned with the company narrative and offerings.

Take a look around your organization with a new perspective, and think about which smart, capable practitioners might be open to partnering more closely with the marketing team. Skim through the internal blogs, lurk in Slack channels or chat tools for other teams, and attend other department town halls to find these hidden gems.

Working with Thought Leaders

As we discussed earlier in this chapter, thought leaders help to build trust and affinity with your audience, and they contribute to long-term business value by influencing revenue, partnerships, recruiting efforts, and market dynamics.

The SMEs and internal influencers discussed in this chapter are an excellent place to look to start building your bench of thought leaders. In many cases, the best way to work with these people is to give them time and resources to experiment and codify their ideas, and more opportunities to share externally on behalf of the brand.

Time to Experiment and Codify New Ideas

It's difficult to show proven results from thought leaders bringing new ideas to the market. The company needs to make a bet that the idea will work and give the thought leader the room to test and iterate, as well as time to document and share throughout the process. Building in public and sharing the development journey is an excellent way for the thought leader to participate in the marketing efforts. If the company wants to show that they take an innovative approach to solving problems, they need to *actually show* that they take an innovative approach!

Sharing the prototypes, talking about the test and optimization cycles, and showcasing the results from internal experiments and customer wins builds credibility and trust. It also helps with change management and idea adoption, since new ideas can be scary. If a person with credibility and a large following brings the audience along on the journey, the new ideas feel more familiar, and the results seem more attainable.

Opportunities to Share Externally

As we discussed in Chapter 9, focusing only on executives is a common pitfall when trying to bring thought leaders into the marketing mix. It means that marketing teams often over-allocate the budget, content creation, and coordination support to executives.

Instead, companies looking to set up a bench of thought leaders should earmark budget for travel and expenses to send up-and-coming thought leaders at all seniority levels to speak at conferences. They should build partnerships with marketing, social media, and communications teams to help amplify that individual's content.

They should also publish the experiments and results on company-owned channels, ensuring that this content receives budget for promotion via paid ads, content syndication, and other distribution channels. If you want to show up as a brand that shares thought leadership, amplifying the employees who create and share new ideas is an excellent way to start.

BRIDGING THE GAP BETWEEN EXISTING CONVERSATIONS AND INNOVATIVE IDEAS

I'm often asked, "How can we distribute our thought leadership content using SEO?" This is a tricky question, because the two types of content are generally at odds. SEO keywords represent the existing conversation and the information people already search for, while thought leadership introduces new concepts and ideas that change the conversation.

Fortunately, incorporating influencers, SMEs, and thought leaders into the marketing mix, along with other tactics, like email, paid ads, and press, can help you bridge the gap between the existing conversation and the new concepts you want to introduce.

For example, consider the following challenge in which we coin a new term that no one's searching for.

Step 1: Identify the existing conversation and rank for those terms.

If you want to *change* the conversation, you must be *in* the conversation first.

- What are the existing sets of problems and solutions?
- What are the indications that existing solutions no longer work?
- Why are those solutions starting to break?

Start by identifying the search terms associated with these questions to understand how your audience talks about the topics in the space. Input from SMEs is valuable during this research phase, since they're solving the problems of the target audience, and speaking with customers and users to help hone the solution.

For example, my playground framework addresses issues with the buyer's journey aligned to the traditional linear funnel (as we learned in Chapter 2). This means that the following terms are relevant to my thought leadership on this topic (not comprehensive, of course):

- Linear funnel
- Buyer's journey
- Awareness, Consideration, Decision
- Funnel stages
- Marketing funnel.

Step 2: Use problem statements in your H2s.

Once you know the existing conversation, you can tweak your headlines to call out the problems with the current thinking, for example:

- Pitfalls of the linear funnel
- Why the funnel is broken
- Go beyond ToFu, MoFu, and BoFu (a funnel's top, middle, and bottom)
- Is the linear funnel dead?
- What to use instead of the linear funnel.

Include a short overview of the existing solution before diving into your unique point of view.

Step 3: Introduce the thought leadership.

Once you tee up the existing conversation and outline why current solutions no longer work, you can dive into your thought leadership content.

If you can name your framework or coin a term, you can start making a play to turn this into an "official" term in the space. An excellent example of this is "zero-click content," or "Zero-Click Marketing," the concept that Amanda Natividad named to describe content for which everything is on the native platform, such as a SERP or social media channel, instead of requiring the reader to click a link to a different site to access the content (see Chapter 6).

Creating content that's optimized for native consumption is not a new concept, but it's hard to talk about "creating content for native consumption in the SERP or feed" every time you want to reference this idea. Amanda coined a quippy and easy-to-understand term for this concept, and now people use her phrase when they discuss the concept.

Step 4: Go beyond SEO articles.

If we continue the example of "zero-click content," we realize that Amanda didn't just rely on slogging it up to the top of the rankings with this term. She has huge audience numbers on X and LinkedIn, and she works with Rand Fishkin, another marketing powerhouse with a strong following on both X and LinkedIn. Together, they shared this term in their content across social media, acting as influencers to amplify the idea. They also shared it via the SparkToro brand channels, including their newsletter, blog, and social media handles.

If you're really looking to redefine a conversation, you could run ads, boost your social media posts, and pay for content syndication to increase awareness of your new concept.

Finally, ask your SMEs to start incorporating the new term or idea into their conversations with internal sales teams, prospects, and customers, and ask your internal influencers to start sharing it when they talk about problems and solutions on their personal channels. The more people hear the concept or term in the context of the problem they're trying to solve, the more likely they are to start using it themselves, sharing it with their network, and, in turn, bringing it into the existing conversation, so that more people start searching for it.

Conclusion

Influencers, subject-matter experts, and thought leaders each add unique value to the marketing mix, helping brands to create content to engage audiences in different ways.

Influencers help you reach a new audience or show up in a new channel. SMEs help you troubleshoot existing problems and implement existing solutions. Both have the potential to become thought leaders if they are willing to dedicate time to growing in the pillars where they are weak. Thought leaders help you introduce new ideas into the market, but true thought leadership requires a significant investment from the individual and the company.

Ask yourself which type of creator you need, based on your goals and existing capabilities, and keep an open mind about who, how, and when to bring each type of creator into your marketing programs.

In the next chapter, we'll look at practical exercises to help interested SMEs and internal influencers grow into thought leaders.

Chapter Summary

- Influencers, SMEs, and thought leaders can all add value to the marketing mix, but each individual offers a different type of impact.

- Take a holistic approach to partnering with internal and external influencers and internal SMEs. These creators have the potential to become thought leaders if they have the desire to invest in growing in each pillar.

- Avoid common pitfalls, including transactional relationships, insisting that creators focus on sharing company-provided content, and trying to turn one type of creator into another.

Note

1 Influencer Marketing Hub (2024) *The State of Influencer Marketing 2024: Benchmark Report*, influencermarketinghub.com/influencer-marketing-benchmark-report (archived at https://perma.cc/55KJ-54YF)

Build Thought Leaders

Leaders

Practical Exercises to Define Narratives, Distribution, and Personal Brand Elements

In order to grow in the four pillars of thought leadership— credibility, profile, prolific, and depth of ideas—you need to hone your narratives across the conceptual, strategic, and tactical depths, and build a personal brand. It takes time and consistent investment to grow in each pillar, so you need to find and track opportunities to write, speak, and engage with your audience.

As we discussed in Chapter 11 on bringing influencers, SMEs, and thought leaders into the marketing mix, you can still have a lot of impact and make a lot of money if you are particularly strong in one or two of the pillars of thought leadership. For example, most people pass through the subject-matter expert (SME) profile and the influencer profile on their journey to thought leadership.

Regardless of where you start, and regardless of where you end up, the ability to refine and share your core ideas and build an audience is essential. I'm often asked if thought leaders are born or made. I expect it comes as no surprise that I resoundingly believe that thought leaders are made—because you can learn the skills required for thought leadership, and you can put in the work to become a thought leader:

- You can learn how to be a strong writer.
- You can improve your public speaking skills.
- You can practice creativity and innovation.

The people who become thought leaders are not innately so much smarter than everyone else or so much more talented than everyone else or so much any other thing than anyone else. They work hard to become thought leaders:

- They practice good habits, in their mind and their routine.
- They refine their processes and use the right tools.
- They build, consistently, over time.

In this chapter, we'll explore key actions and exercises to help you and your colleagues improve in credibility, profile, being prolific, and developing a depth of ideas.

Find and Refine Your Ideas

As noted in Chapter 3 when I introduced the elements of the playground, content strategy that includes defined narratives and distribution channels is key to reaching your audience. These contribute to your depth of ideas and prolific pillars by helping to focus your narrative and consistently publish relevant content. Consider the following questions.

Who is Your Audience

- Are your audience members individual contributors or managers, practitioners or non-practitioners, and what is their seniority?
- What do they already know? Where are the knowledge gaps about the topics/trends/industry you intend to share about?
- What do you want them to do after consuming your content? (Buy something? Share with their network? Apply for a job? Connect with you?)
- Where does your audience spend time and how do they like to consume content (social media platforms, conferences/meet-ups/communities, articles/videos/podcasts)?

What Outcomes Do You Want to Drive?

- Are they business outcomes, such as increasing brand awareness, generating more inbound leads, accelerating deal velocity, and increasing revenue?
- Are they personal outcomes, such as growing your follower count on one or more platforms, sharing your knowledge and being seen as an expert, improving your chances of securing a new job at a target company, or monetizing your content on different channels?

What Are You Willing to Commit to?

- On which channels and platforms and in which communities are you already active (and will commit to staying active)?
- What types of deliverables do you already create, enjoy creating, and will continue to create?
- How much time are you willing and able to spend creating, sharing, and engaging? (Be honest! There's no right answer, only different outcomes.)

Once you have an idea of who you're addressing, what you want to achieve, and how much energy you're willing to devote, it's time to decide where to focus. You can map your talking points to the content depths discussed in Chapter 3:

- **Conceptual:** The what and why of an idea that helps your audience understand the problem space
- **Strategic:** The key knowledge, processes, and tools that must be in place to make the conceptual ideas a reality
- **Tactical:** The step-by-step instructions and ongoing tasks that need to be completed in order to implement the strategy and conceptual ideas.

Collect Topics

If you don't already have a clear idea of your topics, start with an open brainstorm. Grab some sticky notes and a pen or your digital whiteboarding tool of choice, and write down all the topics, ideas, headlines, and angles that come to mind. At this stage, the goal is simply to get all the ideas out of your head. Don't try to filter, edit, or group them just yet.

Once you write down all the ideas, take a walk. Yes, walk away from them! This helps clear your mind and allows the ideas to percolate just a little bit more. You'll come back to your mess of ideas with a clear head, ready to take the next step.

In the next stage, group similar ideas together. At this point, you're still not looking to name the groups or turn them into official categories; you're simply trying to collect similar ideas. If you find that some ideas fit into multiple groups, arrange the groups so that those sticky notes or digital bubbles sit in the middle of two categories. If you see that some ideas or angles don't fit into any group, move them off to the side as stand-alone topics.

At this point, you should start to see some clear groups, with a few areas claiming most of the ideas, and a few ideas that aren't connected to any others. If you find that you're putting all the sticky notes into a single group, take another pass to try to divide that group into a couple of subgroups. Using the guidelines outlined in Chapter 3 for conceptual, strategic, and tactical depths, you should have roughly three or four big groups with five to seven ideas each. If you find that you have more than five groups, take another pass to consolidate or remove some of the ideas. Similarly, if you find that you have fewer than three ideas in a group, take another pass at the one-off sticky notes to see if they fit into a bigger group. If not, move the smallest group of sticky notes to the side for later consideration.

Once you group all of your ideas into categories, take another walk. Again, the goal is to clear your mind and let your subconscious make connections as you walk. Too often, people try to force topics that they think they should talk about, or angles that they think are the "right" ones. In reality, your content won't be successful unless you're passionate and knowledgeable about it. Taking a walk as you go through the ideation process clears out the preconceived notions and gives you space to come back and evaluate your work with fresh eyes.

When you return to your idea groupings, you can evaluate which groups align most with your expertise, audience interest, and goals.

Then, be aware of the following pitfalls to avoid as you start mapping out which topics to commit to.

Don't Get Stuck in a Box of Your Past Experience

Many people think they must talk about what they've done, instead of focusing on what they want to do in the future. The problem is that the more you talk about a subject publicly, the more likely you are to attract attention, questions, and offers related to that topic. Think carefully about what you want in the future, and don't be afraid to focus on what you want to be known for over the next 18 months. If you don't currently have the expertise to share insights in this area, you can turn it into a public learning journey, where you bring people along as you expand your skills or knowledge. The future-oriented mindset can also help you eliminate some of the one-off topics on your list.

For example, early in my career, I managed event logistics and email campaigns. I didn't enjoy either of these areas, and I don't want the majority of my work or conversations to focus on these topics. Thus, I rarely talk about them publicly, and only in the context of a bigger marketing strategy or campaign discussion.

Ensure Topics Have Enough Depth

Remember, the conceptual ideas are meant to fuel your content for 18 to 24 months. This means that you need enough angles, anecdotes, and real-world examples to create content on this topic consistently. If you see a category with only a handful of angles, it might not be broad or deep enough to be a conceptual category.

Ensuring your categories include the right mix of breadth and depth also helps you evaluate future topics. You might be excited about an angle or idea, but if you find that it doesn't fit into any of your current conceptual categories, you'll know that you either need to explore it more to flesh it out or discard it until you generate more insights to share.

Consider the Formats and Channels

As you evaluate each category, think about whether it maps into multiple assets and channels. Pay close attention to whether it maps to the formats you enjoy creating and the channels where you're already active. Some ideas lend themselves to videos. Do you enjoy creating videos? Are you skilled at creating videos? Are you already sharing videos on a platform that rewards video creation? If the answer to these questions is no, you might want to re-evaluate whether that topic is best-suited for your efforts at this time. You might choose to improve your video creation, editing, and distribution skills, but you'll need to dedicate time and resources if you do go down that path. If you aren't excited about an asset or channel, it's much more difficult to stay consistent in it.

For example, I naturally think and create content in a way that resonates on LinkedIn, but I struggle on X. I tend to write in a conversational, educational tone, which works well on LinkedIn, but I'm inconsistent on Instagram, with few discernable patterns in my photos, and no regular publishing schedule. Every so often, I write on the site Medium, but I reserve that space for more philosophical or abstract content. If you stumble on my Medium posts, you might be surprised that I'm the same author you follow on LinkedIn, because the style is so different. If you're just starting to share, pick one or two outlets and formats that you enjoy and which come easily to you (see Figure 12.1). You can always expand them later. Then, once you have honed your ideas into topics and angles, it's time to start creating and sharing!

Figure 12.1   Sample Narratives Mapped to Assets and Distribution Channels

Topic Area	Depth	Angle/Headline	Asset	Outlet
Content in the Buyer's Journey	Conceptual	The Funnel is Dead, Use a Playground Instead	Long article	Contributed blog post
	Strategic	Map Content Depths, Not Funnel Stages	Slide carousel	Personal LinkedIn post
	Tactical	5 Tips to Increase Reach and Conversion	Video	YouTube
Thought Leadership	Conceptual	What is Thought Leadership and Why Does it Matter?	Medium article	Owned blog post
	Strategic	The Four Pillars of Thought Leadership	Presentation	Breakout session at industry conference
	Tactical	How to Discover Your Unique Point of View	Short text	Personal LinkedIn post

Build Your Personal Brand

As you think about creating and distributing your content, you'll want to share in a way that's unique and authentic to you. This is important for a few reasons:

- **Sharing in your authentic voice makes it easier to share regularly**. Staying true to yourself and speaking from your own experience makes it easier to stay consistent because you have a continual influx of new challenges, anecdotes, and examples. You can take inspiration from your everyday experiences, questions you ask and answer, and challenges you solve in your day job or client work.

- **Sharing authentically builds trust**. People trust people like themselves, and it's much easier to build rapport with someone who you feel is being honest. Your audience can find generic, faceless content all over the internet, and they can't make a personal connection if you don't show them the person behind the content. Infusing your personality and personal experience into your content helps your audience believe what you say and gives the sense that they have a relationship with a real person.

- **Sharing in your own voice differentiates your content**. In the age of AI-generated content, everything starts to sound the same, with templated hooks, predictable structure, and generic takeaways. It's difficult to tell who wrote which article. Was it a brand? A specific author? Does it matter? Writing in your own voice makes it clear that it's your ideas, your experience, and your content. People can tell that you created the content.

Unfortunately, some people have an adverse reaction to the recommendation to build a personal brand. They think curating a personal brand means "selling out" to marketing: Read this script. Wear these clothes. Sell this product. The crux of the argument against a personal brand is that you shouldn't turn yourself into a product, because you are not, in fact, a product. You're a person. With thoughts and feelings and messiness, and it's inauthentic to polish yourself up into a "persona" for public consumption.

I would argue though that we present different sides of ourselves to the world every day. The people, the environment, our mood, our goals—these affect who shows up to an interaction. Gym Ashley, Wife Ashley, Friend Ashley, and Work Ashley are all me... but they're different aspects of me. I don't generally bring Gym Ashley to Work, because Gym Ashley is pretty hardcore and intimidating! I want my colleagues to feel comfortable approaching me, collaborating with me, and disagreeing with me. If Work Ashley showed up at the Gym, the personal lifting records would suffer, not least because Work Ashley wears a pencil skirt, heels, and make-up. Interestingly, working from home during the pandemic meant blurring the lines between work selves and home selves for many of us. It's more acceptable in many industries to show up to the virtual morning meeting in gym clothes, see pets peeking into the screen, or stay off-camera to eat lunch during a meeting.

Often, a problem with a "personal brand" is that many people focus so much on the "brand" that they forget the "personal." This is especially true of marketing "ninjas," "gurus," and "rockstars" who claim to be the Lord of LinkedIn or the Purveyor of Paid. We're so good at branding that we box ourselves into a quippy tagline or fancy jargon that no one really understands or cares to understand. We steal from the Instagram lifestyle influencer playbook to create a signature sign-off, perfect palate, and curated content.

If that previous paragraph made you roll your eyes, you're in good company. I don't want to consume the "one thing I need to be awesome" from a marketing ninja either! But, choosing a focus area, using a consistent tone on certain platforms, and showing up as a subset of your whole self does not make you "not a person." Branding is not meant to turn you into a fake robot to shill for something; it's about honing in on the ideas, skills, and experiences that are uniquely you.

This is much harder for people who aren't marketers, storytellers, or communicators by training or trade. As a marketer, it's natural for me to curate how I show up in the world, and I honestly don't think that much about it on a day-to-day basis. When I work with people outside my discipline, however, I find that prescriptive guidance helps them be *more* authentic.

Marketers partner with you to help you tell authentic stories, share your expertise, and pull out the most relevant experiences. We're not here to tell you what to say or how to say it. We're here to help you put *your* message out into the world in a way that resonates with *your* audience.

Practical Ways to Build an Authentic Personal Brand

It might sound counterintuitive to use "build" and "authentic" in the same sentence. Surely, you don't actually need to build something if it's just inherent to who you are? But, as we have noted, some people are not as comfortable drawing lines around which facets of their experience, personality, and knowledge to share regularly with the world.

Thus, I use the following questions to help people think about their personal brand. There are no "correct" answers to these questions. They're meant to be thought-starters to help you hone your authentic brand. The key is consistency, not perfection. It's also helpful to think through these answers when you're just starting out, with a small audience, so that you don't need to backtrack or make significant changes as you grow.

Voice and Tone

- Do I write in long sentences, quippy phrases, or sarcastic fragments?
- Do I aim to be inspirational? Contrarian? Educational?
- Am I academic, formal, conversational, pithy?

Not sure how to find your voice? Start with your biography. Try this exercise: Write your bio as briefly as possible. Then write it as long as possible. Write it arrogantly. Write it humbly. Write it with short, quippy sentences. Write it with long, formal sentences. You'll start to get a sense of which style feels most like you.

For example, my standard one-sentence bio reads: *Ashley Faus is a marketer, writer, and speaker by day, and a singer, actor, and fitness fiend by night.* But, it could say: *Ashley Faus is a seasoned marketer who holds an MBA from the University of Texas at Dallas.*

Pretty different, right? Both bios are factually correct, but they give different signals about my personality and priorities. Your bio is often the first impression for your audience, since it's included in your conference submissions, appears at the top of your social media profiles, and accompanies your article bylines—making it the perfect place to start finding your voice.

Another thought-starter to help you find your voice is: Do you curse? And does that answer change if it's in-person at your workplace, on stage delivering a presentation, or when you're writing a long-form article as opposed to a social media post? Personally, I rarely curse in professional settings, and I don't think I've ever cursed during a public presentation. I know I've re-shared a social post with expletives, but I usually include a disclaimer about the language. I don't often publicly declare these choices, but if you work with me for long enough, you tend to notice that I don't curse in my content.

Tone is different from cursing. Do you write in long sentences, short sentences, a mix? Do you use proper grammar, punctuation, and spelling? How often do you stray from your own rules? For example, I usually write with proper punctuation and spelling, but sometimes I run out of characters on social media, so I swap "and" to "&" with no thought. But swapping "with" to "w/" gives me pause, because I think it's harder to read. Will my audience grasp my message if it's full of abbreviations? Should I break this content into two tweets to make space for all the characters?

I make these decisions subconsciously all the time because I'm "fluent" in my own voice, but I receive questions from colleagues who are new to social media. For example, one colleague wanted to know if it was ok to write, "Excited to share about [topic]!" or if she should write, "I'm excited to share about [topic]!" I advised her that either way is acceptable. She chose to include "I'm" because that felt more like her.

Clothing

- Do I have a signature "look?" (Recall, for example, Steve Jobs' signature black turtleneck.)

- Do I dress formally, casually, somewhere in between?
- Is my style quirky, colorful, neutrals, tailored?

While some industries require specific attire, most conferences and companies give you a lot of leeway to decide how you want to dress. The key is not to be restricted to a specific "uniform," but rather to feel confident and comfortable in your attire. I recommend a few things to keep in mind as you decide on your wardrobe.

First, make sure you have a mix of colors that work with different backgrounds for filming or appearing on stage, preferably in solid colors near your face. Many conferences use navy, black, or light-brown wood backdrops for the stage. If you're wearing a black dress, or a navy shirt and dark denim pants, you blend into the background. This results in the look of a "floating" head and hands, since the background obscures your torso. Tight lines and busy patterns produce odd effects on video, so solid colors are preferable for filming. If your go-to outfit is a black T-shirt and dark jeans, consider adjusting to include a lighter shade of shirt and pants, in case you're presenting against a black or navy background.

Second, consider how you'll handle a microphone. If you wear pants, make sure you have a pocket or sturdy waistband, in case you need to carry the microphone battery pack with you. If you wear a skirt or dress, make sure you have a place to clip the microphone and carry or attach the battery pack.

Third, focus on comfort and the ability to move in different situations. Personally, I like to wear heeled shoes when I present at in-person conferences, but I always ask the organizer about the type of seating if I'm participating in a panel or fireside chat, to inform my clothing and footwear. Many organizers use stools or tall chairs for panels, and it's difficult to climb onto these seats if I'm wearing a skirt and heels! I'm also conscious of my shoes making sounds on the floor if I'm filming and opt for flat shoes if I know I'll be walking on concrete, marble, or other resonant surfaces. I generally wear minimal jewelry when filming or presenting to avoid my earrings hitting an over-the-ear microphone or bracelets making a distracting noise. Your clothing should allow you to walk, gesture, sit, and stand comfortably, without needing to think about every motion or position.

I recommend curating a couple of go-to outfits for presentations and filming situations. It ensures you feel comfortable and look confident in the final pictures and videos.

Your "Full Self"

- Do I share everything or limit my public persona?
- Do I talk regularly about mistakes and failures, both personal and professional, or focus on lessons learned after the fact?
- Do I include my family, friends, and/or hobbies in my public persona? To what extent? (For example, be careful using names, pictures, and anecdotes that make it easy to identify people.)

People also ask where to draw the line on "personal" content. As noted throughout these questions, there is no single right answer to this question. It's more important to be consistent, and to "train" your audience to expect certain types of content.

For example, I like to wear my favorite glittery face mask in the morning before I present an in-person session. I've shared photos while wearing my face mask on LinkedIn, noting that it's a bit of a tradition. This feels on-brand for me, because I frequently share more personal content, including pictures of the cakes I decorate, videos from the gym, and announcements about musical theater performances. As noted in my bio earlier, it's important to me that people know I'm a singer, actor, and fitness fiend, so I include those elements in my content. Some people would never share a picture in gym clothes or wearing a face mask, so it would be out of place if such an image suddenly showed up as a post published from their profile.

Meanwhile, I rarely talk negatively about my co-workers or employer, and I generally don't share negative feelings about hiring processes, compensation, or promotion trends. A rant or diatribe in this vein would seem quite out of place in my feed, although it might be perfectly normal for other people.

Beware that some phrasing is frequently considered "cringey," particularly if the person is constantly being self-deprecating to the point that it seems like a ploy for sympathy, instead of, for example, authentically sharing about overcoming challenges.

SAMPLE PHRASES TO USE FOR AN AUTHENTIC VOICE

You can use the following phrasing pairs to move from an overly self-deprecating tone to a more authentic voice:

- I was just a stupid kid, I had no idea what I was doing. —> This was a problem I had never solved before, so I had to [build skills, do research, find a mentor].

- I made the dumbest choices as I flailed around trying to figure out how to make it work. —> I went through a lot of tests and iterations, and every time something failed, I learned [lesson] for the next attempt.

- I made tons of mistakes, like [insert a million mistakes of all sizes, some of which are quite awkward]. —> I learned [lesson] from two big missteps: [misstep summary + insight] and [misstep summary + insight].

Try to include only one emotion each time:

- I was humbled, honored, and excited to... —> I'm honored to [share, win, join].

- I was scared, doubtful, and nervous... —> It's nerve-wracking to [do the thing]. Here are [tips to overcome your nerves].

It's easy to think that it doesn't matter if you show names and faces of colleagues, friends, and family when you're a small player. What's the harm? Well, as you become more well-known, they too become more well-known. And your colleagues, friends, and family might not want the spotlight. Don't damage relationships and destroy trust by sharing information that those closest to you might not want you to share.

I mitigate this in a few ways. First, I don't tag people unless I ask them first or I'm referencing something they've already published. Second, if I want to talk about a specific situation, I give quite a bit of space between the inciting incident and the post to ensure that it's not easily identifiable or sensitive. Third, I try to wait until I get the same question or see the same situation multiple times, so that it's not tied to a single individual.

In each case, my goal is to protect my friends, family, and colleagues. I never want to embarrass them or call them out, and I'm cognizant of how my public comments might make them feel. Building trust at scale starts with building trust among the individuals closest to you.

As you think about how much to share, remember that the internet is forever. If you publish a post or share it on a podcast, an audience might stumble on it years later.

Accessibility

- Do I give out my personal email address? My company email address?
- Do I accept all invitations to connect on LinkedIn? Do I leave my direct messages open on sites like X?
- How involved am I in mentorship, making introductions, "pick-your-brain" coffee meet-ups, and attending events?

The same caveats are true for giving out your contact information. It's easy to respond to every message when you only receive a few messages each month, but it becomes increasingly difficult to stay in touch with every person as your following grows. Two tactical recommendations to set consistent boundaries from the beginning are to offer office hours and share a consistent, public place to engage.

Office hours allow you to put time limits around giving free advice, and you can conduct these in a format that allows you to adapt the group size as needed. You could offer one-to-one slots on a monthly basis, or group slots at regular intervals.

Similarly, in the early days, you might suggest that people email you if they have questions about your content, but this obligates you to respond to each individual inquiry, which becomes difficult as the messages become more frequent. It's much more manageable to recommend that folks follow you on social media or subscribe to your channel or newsletter as the default mode of connecting with you. Having this consistent public place also gives you the option to direct visitors to your office hours for deeper engagement, while maintaining your boundaries to avoid over-extending yourself.

As you can see, your personal brand is all about finding your voice and sharing authentically. These questions help you decide how to show up in writing, on camera, and in person, with solid boundaries as you grow.

USING NARRATIVES AND PERSONAL BRAND GUIDELINES TO NAVIGATE TRICKY SITUATIONS

As you become more well-known and have more opportunities for media engagements, speaking at conferences, and being a guest on podcasts, you're likely to run into some questions that you'd rather not answer. Documenting your narratives and personal brand guidelines helps you navigate these scenarios and redirect the conversation back to your core ideas.

The following are three examples of tricky questions, along with tactics to help you pivot the conversation:

Prompt: Walk me through your entire career journey or give me all the details about your last role.

Redirect tactic: The common thread.

Sometimes people want to take you down a rabbit hole on your past, but you want to focus on your future. Instead of taking a deep dive, find a few common threads in your journey, and pick the most relevant one to segue into the topic you're excited to share about. Two instances from my own experience:

- I worked across many different industries, so I'm often asked for details about each role. It takes too much time and too many random details to cover each job in each industry. Instead, I say that the common thread is my willingness to fall in love with my audience and their challenges and wins. This helps me direct the conversation back to a bigger idea that is more likely to dovetail with one of my conceptual ideas.

- I participate in several different hobbies, so interviewers frequently ask how I do so many different activities. Time management, productivity tips, and calendar management are not part of my core narratives, so I generally don't want to focus on this topic in this way.

Instead, I share that the common thread is around energy management rather than nitty-gritty "hacks" for time management.

Prompt: Someone wants to dive into the tactical details about an area where you don't have much experience or you're no longer executing day to day.

Redirect tactic: Up-level.

If you truly have zero experience, it's fine to say so and move on. And, if you're trying to up-level the conversation, say so! Phrases include, "I'd like to zoom out a bit to talk about...," "I think we need to answer the broader question first...," and "Let's up-level this a bit to talk about...."

For example, I frequently receive questions about which specific tools to use for different tasks. The problem is usually that they want a single tool to solve all the problems, or it's framed as using a tool to solve a problem that actually requires better communication, practices, and measurement. The up-level pivot works well to reframe the discussion around criteria to use to evaluate solutions or framing the problem correctly versus a long list of tools.

Prompt: Someone asks about a strategy, tactic, or tool that conflicts with the core of your entire presentation.

Redirect tactic: Ask the right question.

This one is a little tricky, but, sometimes, you need to completely pivot. I've done this a few times, even saying, "I think that's the wrong question. Instead, I would ask [question I think is relevant], so that we can [give a benefit that is relevant]." You need to say it with a smile and a neutral-to-positive tone. It can't come across as an attack or a duck-and-cover, and you must pivot to a relevant topic or tactic.

For example, when I present the playground framework, people tend to ask pointed questions about how to gate content. I'm generally opposed to gating most content, so I don't want to give out tips to gate content! Instead, my pivot is usually along the lines of rethinking attribution and how to report up the impact of content marketing work. The "wrong" question is, "Which content can I gate in the playground?" The pivot is, "Let's think about how you're tracking progress and reporting on your impact." This allows me to talk about content at the strategic and tactical depths in a way that aligns with my conceptual idea about using a playground analogy instead of the linear funnel. I share about how to use different metrics, along with real-world examples of matching the right metrics to each channel and asset.

Grow Your Opportunities to Write and Speak

Being a thought leader means you regularly share insights with an external audience. Speaking engagements, podcast interviews, and bylines are proof-points in the profile and prolific pillars. So, how do you increase the quantity and quality of these opportunities?

You need to be prolific to become prolific! It's a strange situation because you must start sharing and showing up before you get invited to share and show up (in bigger, more prestigious venues). Sometimes, people push back on my insistence that you need to write, record, and engage via owned channels before you start pitching external channels. "No one comments on my LinkedIn posts," "No one visits my blog," "No one watches my YouTube videos." But, they will *never* comment, visit, or watch if you never post!

Most of us don't go viral on our first share. Most of us don't debut on the biggest stage. Most of us don't 10x our followers in a month.

Start commenting.

Start writing.

Start recording.

The more you share, the more people will see that you're smart, engaging, and credible. They want to learn from you, and they want to amplify your ideas.

Sharing on Social Media and Contributing Bylines

I'm blunt about being prolific, because this pillar is entirely in your control. You need to create content and share regularly. There's no shortcut to sharing—you must do it if you want to grow. But people get tripped up on being prolific because they think it means creating long-form content in every channel. This is incorrect; you can start with short content in a single channel. As we discussed in Chapter 4 on creating modular content, you can reuse, repackage, and republish your existing content, adapting the content depth and the asset type across your channels.

The following sentence-starter prompts can help you begin creating original content, based on your real-world experience and expertise:

- I answered this question today:
- I asked this question today:
- Today I'm working on...
- Today I'm thinking about...
- I read this article about...
- I attended this presentation about...

These prompts can take you in many different directions, mapping them into the conceptual, strategic, and tactical depths that you outlined earlier.

For example, I often post about questions I receive using the hashtag #AskAshleyFaus on LinkedIn. I share the question, and answer using the hashtag #AshleyFausAnswers. This makes it easy for me and my audience to reference other questions and answers, and allows me to pull in previous posts about the content. I often include excerpts from previous presentations and links to long-form articles on the topic.

This also helps me generate more ideas in the future. I can look through the #AskAshleyFaus posts for any common threads in the questions and use them as fodder for a new framework or template. For example, I realized that I received a lot of questions about how I secured speaking engagements and contributed bylines, so I wrote a long-form article about tips to pitch. I have adapted and expanded that information into content for a section later in this chapter.

You can also ask for input from your audience if you're stuck in a creative rut. The following engagement prompts can help you start a conversation with your audience, which also helps generate comments for you to respond to:

- Anyone else working on a similar problem?
- How are you tackling this problem?
- What else have you seen on this topic?
- Who else do you know that shares about this topic?
- What insights can you share about this subject?

I find that my audience members share excellent tips, articles, and videos when I ask for more details. It's important to actually consume the content your audience shares with you and engage in conversation via comments and direct messages. This type of engagement prompt aims to help you create genuine connections and find more information. It's not meant as a hack to generate fluffy comments.

Most people write answers to these questions and prompts in their internal chat applications or shared documents. With a few tweaks to anonymize the people involved or generalize the core problem, you can repurpose content like that into a social media post, long-form article, or anecdote in a live speaking engagement.

Remember that being prolific is *not* about writing a 5,000-word opus every single day. It's about habitually creating, sharing, and engaging with your audience.

Writing, recording, and publishing regularly also helps you build credibility and improve your profile to help secure speaking engagements. When I first started out, I published marketing content on my personal blog multiple times each week. I used my personal blog as my portfolio to pitch for guest bylines. I stumbled on a site that hadn't quite launched yet, The Daily Muse, and asked if it needed writers. My consistent publishing showed that I could write well and often, and I ended up publishing multiple articles on the site. It eventually rebranded to The Muse and became quite popular and well-known. In fact, it formed syndication partnerships with sites like Mashable, Time, and Forbes, and my articles ended up being published in these outlets after first running on The Muse.

That initial round of publishing helped give me the credibility to land my first speaking engagements. I started small, delivering talks to two women-in-business groups as part of their monthly lunch-and-learn series. There were only about 15 people in the audience, and they compensated me for my time with a free lunch. These small initial wins gave me something to cite when I pitched for my first in-person conference session.

The key takeaway? Take the small gigs when you're just starting out. It helps you hone your skills and topics into a concise presentation, and demonstrates that you are consistently sharing and engaging.

Create Your Conference Pitch Materials

Many people don't realize that in order to deliver a session in person at a conference, you need to pitch to speak. The call for speakers usually opens three to six months ahead of the conference. This is why I recommend creating your abstract, key takeaways, headshot and bio during the narrative development and personal branding phases of your thought leadership journey. Most conferences require these materials as part of the pitch, with similar requirements for word- and character-count as follows.

Title

The title is usually between 50 and 75 characters long, including spaces. Make sure your title is clear and catchy, but not too clever. Remember, attendees skim the agenda, trying to choose among multiple sessions, so your title should pique their interest. Don't make the mistake of trying to appear so clever that you obscure the actual topic and benefits for your audience.

These are some of the titles I've used in conference sessions about the frameworks shared in this book:

- Beyond the Editorial Calendar: New Rules of Content Strategy
- The Funnel is Dead, Use a Playground Instead
- The New Rules of Social Media
- Fast-Track to Thought Leadership

Abstract

The abstract is usually between 450 and 900 characters long, including spaces. It's meant to tell the audience what they'll learn in the session. It should give a short overview of the problem space and include some information about the new solution that you will introduce during the session. Again, don't try to be too coy with your audience. They skim the abstract quickly as they build their agenda, so you need to ensure they understand that your content is relevant and useful for them.

Here's an example of an abstract I wrote for my talk on thought leadership:

Everybody wants to be an influencer. A spokesperson. A thought leader. Individuals want to build their personal brands, companies want to build their reputation in their industry, and marketers everywhere want to leverage these people and brands to influence customers and job candidates. But what makes a "thought leader?" How do you go from unknown to unstoppable? How can you accelerate the increase in influence and turn it into a repeatable process to build a pipeline of credible spokespeople? In this session, we'll explore strategies, tactics, and real-world success stories of starting from scratch and scaling a thought leadership platform.

Key Takeaways

The key takeaways or learning objectives are usually formatted as bullet points, with roughly 100 characters available for each line. They're meant to showcase the practical and immediately actionable tips the audience will learn during the session. If you plan to share exercises, templates, or frameworks during the presentation, call these out in the key takeaways.

The following examples are a few key takeaways I include when sharing the thought leadership framework:

- Benefits of building and scaling a thought leadership program, both as an individual and an organization
- Framework for building thought leaders: Four pillars to assess and execute a thought leadership strategy
- Strategies, tactics, and real-world examples of building thought leaders within an organization.

Biography and Headshot

Most conferences ask you to include a short biography and a high-resolution headshot. The bio ranges in length from 25 to 75 words, so I recommend writing a couple of different lengths when you complete the bio exercise as part of finding your voice. Your headshot should be current, and I generally recommend submitting a color version, with a bit of extra padding around your face. If the conference wants to do any graphic treatments on it, like changing it to black and white or adding a frame, a color version gives them the flexibility to adapt it to their visual style.

Securing and Tracking Opportunities

Now that you have narrowed down your topics and created materials to pitch, it's time to find relevant outlets. I like to keep track of my pitches, topics, and acceptance rate in a spreadsheet (an example is given in Figure 12.2).

Figure 12.2   Conference Pitch Tracking Spreadsheet

Outlet	Topic	Link	Date	Format	Pitch	Outcome
Sample Name 1	Content Strategy	Sample URL 1	Date 1	Byline	Pitched	Accepted
Sample Name 2	Thought Leadership	Sample URL 2	Date 2	Podcast	Inbound	Declined
Sample Name 3	Social Media Spectrum	Sample URL 3	Date 3	Breakout	Pitched	Rejected
Sample Name 4	Content Strategy	Sample URL 4	Date 4	Panel	Inbound	No Response
Sample Name 5	Social Media Spectrum	Sample URL 5	Date 5	Webinar	Pitched	Rejected
Sample Name 6	Thought Leadership	Sample URL 6	Date 6	Featured Contributor	Inbound	Accepted

First, make a list of 10 publications that are relevant to your audience and topics where you'd like your byline to appear. Focus on outlets that are relevant for your niche, not just on famous publications that everyone reads. Particularly when you're starting out, you're unlikely to secure placements in publications like *Harvard Business Review*, *The Wall Street Journal*, or *The New York Times*. For sites that accept guest contributions, there's usually a dedicated space on the website with editorial guidelines, pitch requirements and contacts, and topics they like to include. Add the link and contact information to your spreadsheet, noting which of your topics are most relevant.

Second, make a list of 10 conferences where you would like to present. If this is your first time speaking at an in-person conference, I recommend focusing on smaller conferences in your industry or topic niche. They usually have a space on the website titled "Call for Proposals," "Call for Speakers," or "Speak at [Conference Name]," which includes details about deadlines, topics, and abstract guidelines. I like to batch the task of finding and inputting all the key dates for relevant conferences to ensure I'm aware of pitch deadlines and know that the conference dates work with my schedule. Add this information to your spreadsheet, with notes about which of your topics are relevant to each conference.

Third, make a list of influencers and SMEs in your field who you want to connect with on social media. You might choose people who are regular speakers at some of your target conferences, editors or journalists at your target publications, or people with an engaged following in your topic areas. Follow their primary social media handles, read or watch their long-form work, and engage with their content by reacting and commenting. The primary goal is to build the relationship and exchange ideas. This step is not meant to hack the algorithm or spam a well-known person. You need to remember that there's a human behind the screen, and you're looking to build trust and rapport with that person. I recommend choosing people who are a couple of steps ahead of you in the journey rather than focusing on the most high-profile names or largest following.

Once you make a list of targets, use the materials you created in the previous step to pitch your content. You can use the same spreadsheet to add the date when you send your pitch, and include the outcome in the spreadsheet as well, noting "accepted," "rejected," or "no response" to your pitch. I also like to include "declined" for opportunities that I don't wish to pursue.

Tracking pitches helps you understand which topics resonate, and helps you iterate on your pitch materials to increase your acceptance rate. It also helps you understand when you're moving up in the profile pillar, since the quantity and quality of outlets that feature your content are proof-points of progress in that pillar.

Conclusion

Becoming a thought leader requires time and consistent work to develop and share ideas. Track your progress by working through each pillar every six months or so, noting your bylines and press mentions, virtual and in-person speaking opportunities, and follower and engagement growth on social media.

As you grow, use inputs such as comments on social posts, questions from interviewers, and problems you solve each day to evolve your narratives at the conceptual, strategic, and tactical depths.

Chapter Summary

- Find your baseline by scoring yourself on the four pillars of thought leadership—credibility, profile, prolific, and depth of ideas.

- Refine your narratives by brainstorming and grouping your ideas, mapping them into the conceptual, strategic, and tactical content depths.

- Build your personal brand by answering questions about your voice and tone, clothing, your full self, and accessibility. Remember, there are no right answers, and being consistent as you grow is most important.

- Be prolific to be prolific! Write, speak, and share on social media regularly, using the narratives and personal brand guidelines you created.

- Track your opportunities to understand which topics resonate most with various audiences, and to understand your progress towards becoming a thought leader.

Conclusion 13

Connect with the Humans Behind the Screen to Accelerate Sales and Increase Customer Retention

I started my undergraduate degree as a musical theater major. I was passionate about singing, acting, and performing in live theater. I knew it would be a difficult career path, but I was excited to begin my studies.

Unfortunately, I experienced a medical issue with my vocal cords, which meant I missed my final exams at the end of my first semester. The doctor told me that I needed to go on vocal rest, which meant I couldn't sing, or speak, for over a month.

I started reflecting on my career trajectory. I didn't really have the talent to perform for a living, and I didn't have the desire to teach. And what if my vocal cords didn't recover? I might not have the option to sing, even if I wanted to continue this professional path!

So, during the search for a new major, I walked into a Marketing 101 class. The opening line of the textbook read, "Marketing is about people." I shut the book and declared my new major that same day, and I've been a marketer ever since.

This fundamental principle has shaped my practice of marketing for more than a decade. It's informed my strategy, tactics, and now, my frameworks. I truly believe that we must connect with the humans that make up our audience. They're not just targets, prospects, personas or the ideal customer profile, or a total addressable market. They're real people, with real problems, seeking real solutions.

This means that my job as a marketer is to match problems with solutions for people. Yes, I need to sell my offering profitably, but, without this core conviction, I won't be able to build long-term trust, affinity, and ultimately, repeatable revenue.

Keys to Connecting with People

We've talked a lot about marketing frameworks, strategy, and tactics throughout this book. Ultimately, though, we need to focus on connecting with the humans behind the screen, which requires:

- Curiosity
- Motivation
- Connection.

Curiosity is about being interested in a person or idea. It's not enough to investigate pain-points for potential customers or users, we need to be curious about our audience members as whole humans. As we think about building the playground to create a delightful, seamless, and impactful journey, we need to understand the narratives that resonate with our audience. What types of content and formats do they enjoy? How can we capture their attention, entertain or fascinate them, and ultimately, help them?

Motivation is about understanding what makes our audience do what they do. Are they striving to grow in their career? Do they want to be more famous or recognized in their industry? Are they seeking more work-life balance? Their underlying drivers help us better articulate how our solutions can help them achieve their goals. That might mean we exchange value through learn-intent content, hiring, strategic partnerships, amplification, or purchases. It's not just about their short-term motivation to potentially buy our offering, it's about their core motivations and how we can exchange value in the long run.

Connection is about building relationships, trust, and rapport. Too often, companies think that connection simply means building a following or sending nurture campaigns to prospects, customers, and users. Instead, brands need to take a holistic approach to connecting by uniting online and offline conversations, helping people become thought leaders, and acknowledging the milestones in the lives of their audiences.

Uniting the Playground, Social Media Spectrum, and Four Thought Leadership Pillars

The playground, social media spectrum, and four pillars of thought leadership work together to help build trust, add value to the audience, and drive revenue for the business.

In order to reach the humans behind the screen, we structure the journey like a playground, focusing on content depths, intent, and time horizons. As we think about who creates and shares the content, we assess and partner with subject-matter experts, influencers, and thought leaders. We then map each asset into different channels, including branded social media handles and personal channels. These tactics help us show the audience that we have people just like them, experiencing and solving similar problems, chasing similar goals, and bringing similar expertise to their work.

This focus on building trust helps drive value in the long run, allowing companies to expand their customer base and the total revenue from each account.

REAL-WORLD EXAMPLE   How Adobe Uses Experiences
to Increase Customer Retention

Adobe is a software-as-a-service provider that created popular design products including Photoshop and Illustrator, and grew to encompass many different digital experiences.

It took a unique approach to a portion of the customer journey that is traditionally associated with bottom-of-funnel or post-purchase phases: Customer success. Adobe realized that tossing the customer over to a separate team after acquisition and conversion was hurting the customers and the bottom line.

In 2018, the company set out to improve its customer success practice, moving beyond up-sell and cross-sell motions, and thinking holistically about driving customer value.[1] To start, it needed to unite all of its business units, assets, and channels. Instead of silos of teams chasing customers from multiple angles, it brought teams together to create a comprehensive customer journey strategy and system of measurement. They mapped out pre- and post-sale touchpoints to understand exactly how each customer moved through the journey.

Instead of focusing on traditional metrics that solely benefit the company, like renewal rates, Adobe focused on metrics that indicated a positive customer outcome, with a more holistic understanding of the value added throughout the customer journey. For example, the teams included metrics like usage, which indicate that the customer is spending time in the product, and hopefully, getting value. They also included metrics like support requests and escalations to track when customers were blocked.

The teams also dedicated executive-level owners to each stage of the journey to ensure that the work was prioritized, and all decisions had a final approver. This allowed them to maximize collaboration for the good of the user, instead of getting stuck in individual silos.

To manage the transformation and associated metrics, Adobe created a platform to give an end-to-end view of each customer, which allows the teams to tailor the experiences. Adobe has now released a version of that technology to help its customers improve the experience they offer to their customers. It's a virtuous cycle of customer-focused decisions and metrics in the playground-style journey.

Building trust and exchanging value are constant pursuits. While technology has helped us scale bigger, create and distribute faster, and track with more granularity, it can't replace the human-to-human connect. In the age of AI, it's becoming more difficult to know who to trust.

People are looking for the people like themselves. As marketers, let's help show our audience that we're people they can trust.

Note

1 Long, M. (2020) How We Changed the Customer Success Conversation at Adobe, Adobe Experience Cloud Blog, November 2, business.adobe. com/blog/perspectives/how-we-changed-the-customer-success-conversation-at-adobe (archived at https://perma.cc/NZK9-EMWD)

INDEX

Note: Page numbers in *italics* refer to figures.

Looking for another book?

Explore our award-winning
books from global business
experts in Marketing and Sales

Scan the code to browse

www.koganpage.com/marketing

More books from Kogan Page

ISBN: 9781398611504

ISBN: 9781398608436

ISBN: 9781398612976

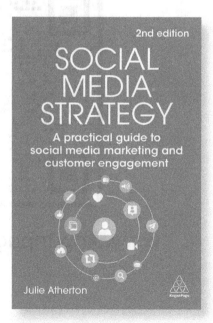

ISBN: 9781398609990

www.koganpage.com

From 4 December 2025 the EU Responsible Person (GPSR) is:
eucomply oÜ, Pärnu mnt. 139b – 14, 11317 Tallinn, Estonia
www.eucompliancepartner.com